A Description of Moldavia

Dimitrie Cantemir
Prince of Moldavia
1693, 1710-1711

Dimitrie Cantemir

A Description of Moldavia

Edited, with an introduction by A.K. Brackob

The Center for Romanian Studies
Las Vegas ◊ Chicago ◊ Palm Beach

Published in the United States of America by
Histria Books
7181 N. Hualapai Way, Ste. 130-86
Las Vegas, NV 89166 USA
HistriaBooks.com

The Center for Romanian Studies is an independent academic and cultural institute with the mission to promote knowledge of the history, literature, and culture of Romania in the world. The publishing program of the Center is affiliated with Histria Books. Contributions from scholars from around the world are welcome. To support the work of the Center for Romanian Studies, contact us at info@centerforromanianstudies.com.

All rights reserved. No part of this book may be reprinted or reproduced or utilized in any form or by any electronic, mechanical or other means, now known or hereafter invented, including photocopying and recording, or in any information storage or retrieval system, without the permission in writing from the Publisher.

Library of Congress Control Number: 2021945379

ISBN 978-1-59211-025-4 (hardcover)
ISBN 978-1-59211-400-9 (s0ftbound)
ISBN 978-1-59211-268-5 (eBook)

Copyright © 2024 by Histria Books

Contents

Introduction 7

Part I – Geography 15

    Chapter I – About the Past and Present Names of Moldavia 17

    Chapter II – About the Location of Moldavia, Its Past and Present Borders, and the Local Climate 20

    Chapter III – About the Waters of Moldavia 25

    Chapter IV – About the Counties and Towns of Moldavia 31

    Chapter V – About the Mountains and Minerals of Moldavia 50

    Chapter VI – About the Fields and Forests of Moldavia 55

    Chapter VII – About the Wildlife and Domestic Animals of Moldavia 59

Part II – Politics 65

    Chapter I – About the Organization of the Moldavian State 67

    Chapter II – About the Election of the Rulers of Moldavia 73

    Chapter III – Ancient and Present Customs Regarding the Enthronement of the Princes of Moldavia 85

    Chapter IV – About the Acknowledgment of the Ruler 108

    Chapter V – About the Removal of Rulers from the Throne 114

    Chapter VI – About the Boyars of Moldavia and their Ranks 123

    Chapter VII – About the Army of Moldavia 139

Chapter VIII – About Court Ceremonies during the Ruler's
Outings and Feasts 144

Chapter IX – About the Royal Hunts 152

Chapter X – About Royal Funerals 154

Chapter XI – About the Laws of Moldavia 157

Chapter XII – About the Seat of Judgment of the Ruler
and the Boyars 159

Chapter XIII – About Moldavia's Income in Past
and Present Times 166

Chapter XIV – About the Tributes and Gifts that Moldavia
Pays to the Ottoman Court 170

Chapter XV – About the Moldavian Nobility 175

Chapter XVI – About the Other Inhabitants of Moldavia 185

Chapter XVII – About the Customs of Moldavia 192

Chapter XVIII – About Engagements and Weddings in Moldavia .. 200

Chapter XIX – About Funerals in Moldavia 207

Part III – Religion and Literature 211

Chapter I – About the Religion of Moldavia 213

Chapter II – About the Church Hierarchy 221

Chapter III – About the Monasteries of Moldavia 226

Chapter IV – About the Language of Moldavia 228

Chapter V – About Moldavian Letters 234

Index 239

Introduction

A *Description of Moldavia* is a unique piece of historical literature. Written by one of Moldavia's most illustrious rulers, it provides an account of the principality giving readers an understanding of the geography, history, and culture of this historic Romanian land. There is little else like it in Romanian historical writing. It is a valuable resource for anyone with an interest in Romanian history, but also for those seeking to understand the inner workings of a small European principality in the medieval and early modern era.

Moldavia was founded in the mid-fourteenth century under Bogdan I (c. 1359-1365, called *Întemeietorul*, meaning the Founder), a voivode from Maramureș. Stretching from the eastern Carpathians, Moldavia bordered the Siret, the Dniester, the Black Sea, and the Danube. The fifteenth century marked a Golden Age for the principality, during the reigns of two distinguished rulers: Alexander the Good (1400-1432) and his grandson, Stephen the Great (1457-1504), a cousin of the famous prince of neighboring Wallachia, Vlad III Dracula.

Dimitrie Cantemir, the author of *A Description of Moldavia*, was one of the most erudite princes in the storied history of the principality. He was a distinguished historian, philosopher, musicologist, composer, linguist, geographer, ethnographer, and novelist.

Cantemir claimed that his family was of Tartar origin, having settled in Moldavia in the fourteenth century, and that the family played an important role in the principality already during the reign of Stephen the Great (1457-1504). These claims have been disputed by scholars. His father, Prince Constantine (1685-1693), adopted the name Cantemir. A popular ruler, Constantine Cantemir was not a highly-educated man. His subjects considered him a man of the people and he was known as a devout Christian.

Dimitrie was born Dumitrașcu Cantemir to Constantine and his third wife, Ana Bantăș, on October 26, 1873. When his father took the throne as prince of Moldavia in 1685, he had to send one of his two sons to the Porte as a hostage as was customary at the time. This fell upon his eldest son, Antioch, 16, who went to Istanbul, while 12-year-old Dimitrie remained at the royal court in Iași, the capital of Moldavia. Dimitrie displayed an affinity for learning from a young age. While he received a traditional education at court, his father also had him tutored by a monk named Ieremia Cacavalas, one of Moldavia's most distinguished scholars.

In 1688, Dimitrie took the place of Antioch as a hostage at the Porte. While there, he learned the Turkish language, history, and customs. After three years in Istanbul, he returned to Moldavia in 1791, replaced again at the Porte by his brother, Antioch. He spent the next few years in Iași until the death of his father. Having reached the age of 17, he began to take part in affairs of state. In September 1692, he participated, alongside his father, in the campaign with the Ottomans to retake the fortress of Soroca that had been occupied by the Poles. Soon after, in February 1692, Constantine fell ill with kidney disease. With his father ill, Dimitrie presided over the joint visit of three Patriarchs — Iacov from Constantinople, Dionisie from Jerusalem, and

Gherasim from Alexandria. The principality had received this honor because of the pious reputation of Constantine Cantemir.

Constantine died on 13 or 17 March 1693 at the age of 81. In accordance with the customs of the country, the boyars elected his son Dimitrie, who had earned their respect and admiration, as the new prince. The Sultan, however, did not confirm his election. Instead, Constantine Duca, son-in-law of Wallachian Prince Constantine Brâncoveanu, was appointed Prince after the requisite bribes had been paid at the Porte. This marked another moment in the ongoing conflict between the Cantemirs and Brâncoveanus that caused much unrest in the Romanian principalities and led to frequent changes on the throne. The intrigues continued and, in 1696, Duca was replaced by Dimitrie's elder brother Antioch, who ruled Moldavia from 1696-1700, before being replaced again by Duca. Antioch ruled again from 1705-1707. During most of this time, Dimitrie remained in Istanbul where he continued his studies and remained active in diplomatic life in the Ottoman capital.

Dimitrie had returned to Moldavia during the reign of his brother. A marriage with Cassandra, the daughter of Wallachian prince Şerban Cantacuzino, a rival of Constantine Brâncoveanu, was arranged. The couple married in Iaşi on May 9, 1699. Shortly after, Dimitrie returned to Istanbul with Cassandra where they lived in a lavish palace that she had inherited from her father. In the Ottoman capital, Dimitrie remained attuned to international affairs while he continued his study of the Turkish language and history. The resources available in the Imperial capital to a man of his scholarly inclinations afforded him the opportunity to do research for books that he was planning to write. In 1705, he wrote the first Romanian language novel, *Historia Hieroglyphica*.

After the failed siege of Vienna in 1683, the Ottoman Empire was a power in decline. Meanwhile, Russia, under Peter the Great, was a rising power after his victory over Charles XII of Sweden. Cantemir, who dreamed of independence for his principality, saw this and he realized that the autonomy he sought depended on the weakening of Ottoman power. As tensions grew between Russia and the Ottoman Empire, the Porte looked to make a change in Moldavia. The Ottomans realized that Moldavia would become the primary battlefield between the two rival empires and they wanted a reliable prince on the throne, but one that also had the support of the native population. Dimitrie Cantemir seemed like the perfect choice. His political and diplomatic acumen, along with his popularity led the Grand Vizier to secure his appointment as Prince in 1710, without having to pay tribute at the Porte as was customary.

While all this was going on, the Swedish King Charles XII took refuge in Moldavia at Varnița, near the fortress of Tighina creating a political and diplomatic crisis between the Russian and Ottoman empires. Peter the Great demanded that Charles XII be turned over to him or expelled. This served as the pretext for war for the ambitious Russian Tsar. Cantemir arrived in Iași on December 10, 1710. The newly-appointed Moldavian Prince initially supported the Ottomans, providing them with intelligence on Russian troop movements. Secretly, however, Dimitrie planned to aid the Tsar as he believed this would be the best way to secure the autonomy of his principality. He entered into secret negotiations with Peter the Great and, on April 13, 1711, he signed a treaty of alliance with Russia at Luck.

The terms of the Treaty of Luck were very favorable for Moldavia. The Russian Tsar recognized the Dniester River as the historic border between Moldavia, as well as Moldavian control over Bugeac. In addition, the Tsar confirmed Cantemir's rule for life and hereditary rule for his ancestors. The treaty also provided that if Russia lost the upcoming war with the Ottomans, forcing Cantemir to flee the principality, he would then receive estates in Russia and an Imperial allowance. Unfortunately, in 1812, Imperial Russia and the Soviet Union in 1940 and 1944, both infringed upon the territorial integrity of this Romanian land, and the portion of Moldavia east of the Prut River fell under Russian and later Soviet occupation. Since the fall of the Soviet Union, the Republic of Moldova has emerged on part of this land as an independent state, but a portion of the territory historically belonging to Moldavia as described by Cantemir still remains within the borders of modern Ukraine.

The Treaty of Luck remained secret until the Turks entered Bugeac. Cantemir waited for Peter the Great's troops to cross the Dniester in the summer of 1711 before he openly declared for Russia and rallied the country against the Ottomans. He greeted Peter the Great at Țuțora and then proceeded to Iași where they planned for the upcoming battle with the Turks. The Ottomans, however, moved more rapidly than expected and caught the Russians unprepared at the battle of Stănilești that took place from July 18-22, 1711, where the Tsar suffered a humiliating defeat. The situation now desperate, Cantemir returned to Iași ahead of the Ottomans and took Cassandra and his six children — Matei, Constantin, Șerban, Antioch, Maria, and Smaradga — and their belongings and began the long retreat into exile, along with many of the boyars who had supported him.

True to his word to his Moldavian ally, Peter issued a unique decree on August 1, 1711, granting Dimitrie Cantemir the title of Serene Highness and gave him jurisdiction over his subjects in exile, further decreeing that he was answerable only to the Tsar. He stayed in Kiev for a time; then, in 1713, he was granted two houses in Moscow along with nearby villages. Shortly after, tragedy struck when his beloved wife Cassandra died on May 12, 1713. This was a great loss to him and he suffered from depression.

After Cassandra's death, he lived a quiet secluded life and occupied himself with his studies. Cantemir was described as a man of medium build, "rather lean than fat. He had an agreeable countenance and always spoke with affability, mildness, and caution. His custom was to rise at five in the morning, and, smoking a pipe of tobacco over a dish of coffee after the Turkish manner, he retired to his study till dinner, which was constantly at noon. He generally dined upon one dish, his favorite dish being small chicken with sorrel. At his meals he always drank water with his wine. Drunkenness was his mortal enemy, for, after once drinking too much, he was sick a fortnight. He slept a little after dinner, and the rest of the day was spent in his study until seven in the evening. Then he saw his family, and, supping at ten, he went to bed at twelve."[1]

Cantemir's reputation as a distinguished scholar led him to be elected as a member of the Berlin Academy in 1714. During these years, he wrote *A Description of Moldavia* and his history of Ottoman Empire, among other works. Still, he dreamed of one day returning to Moldavia and he continued to lobby the Tsar for action against the Turks to free the Romanian lands, where the Greek-Phanariot regime had been installed, but without success.

On January 14, 1717, at the age of 46, he married Anastasia, the 16-year-old daughter of a Russian Prince Ivan Trubestskoy. She was considered one of the great beauties of her time and admired for her

---

[1] Demetrius Cantemir, *A history of the growth and decay of the Othman Empire*... (London, 1735), p. 459.

remarkable intellect, having studied in Sweden. Despite their age difference, they seemed like a perfect match. Cantemir moved to St. Petersburg where he became actively involved in the social life of the Russian capital while continuing his scholarly work. The couple had one daughter, Ekaterina Smaradga Cantemir, born in 1720. The demands of societal life in the capital, however, led him into debt. Once again, he appealed to the Tsar for help, which Peter did not deny him. The former Prince received the title of personal counselor to the Tsar and became a member of the Imperial Senate. In the summer of 1722, he accompanied Peter the Great on his expedition to Persia. Cantemir fell ill on this trip and had to remain in Astrakhan until he recovered enough to return to his estates near Moscow in January 1723.

The illness had visibly so weakened the former Moldavian Prince that friends could hardly recognize him. Cantemir's final days were difficult. In addition to poor health, he was also nearly bankrupt. Knowing his end was near, he wrote to his personal secretary: "My health grows weaker each day. I am in desperate need of money... If then end of life is coming there will be nothing to bury me with."[2] He never fully recovered his health and he died on August 21, 1723. His dream of one day returning to his native Moldavia, however, was eventually fulfilled. In 1935, his body was exhumed and his remains returned to Romania where he was interred at the Three Hierarchs Church in Iași where he rests today.

A Description of Moldavia is perhaps his most important work as it provides a unique insight into the history and customs of the land written by one of its rulers. The work was originally written in Latin

---

[2]Quoted in Dimitrie Cantemir, *Descrierea Moldovei*, ed. Gheorghe Adamescu (București: Editura Cartea Românească, 1942), p. 27.

at the request of his fellow members of the Academy in Berlin. It remained in manuscript form until after his death. His son Antioch took it with him to London and later to Paris where he served as an ambassador of the Russian Tsar. When Antioch died in Paris in 1744 with no heirs, his belongings were sold at auction. The manuscript then passed through several hands until I.L. Redslob, a professor in Berlin, translated it into German and published it in *Magazin für die neue Historie und Geographie*.[3] In 1771, it first appeared as a separate volume, under the title *Demetrii Kantemirs ehemaligen Fürsten der Moldau, historisch-geographisch und politsche Beschreibung der Moldau* in Frankfurt and Leipzig. *A Description of Moldavia* was first published in a Romanian language edition at the Monastery of Neamț in 1825 and has since appeared in various Romanian language translations. The present volume, however, represents the first time this important work appears in an English-language translation. It includes Cantemir's remarkable map of Moldavia, one of the earliest detailed cartographic depictions of the Romanian Principality.

I would like to thank Diana Livesay for her work on the translation and for her help in preparing this important book. Footnotes marked *Author's Note* are Cantemir's original notes. All others have been added to this edition. *A Description of Moldavia* is part of the ongoing work of the Center for Romanian Studies to promote knowledge of the history, literature, and culture of Romania in the world.

A.K. Brackob

---

[3] *Magazin für die neue Historie und Geographie*, parts III and IV, 1769-1770.

Part I
Geography

Chapter I
About the Past and Present Names of Moldavia

The whole of Moldavia, as we now call it, together with the western regions, was once under the domination of the Scythians, who, although they conquered more than three-quarters of the world, did not have a stable settlement due to their nomadic nature. Following the arrival of various nomadic groups, who left their mark on these lands and gave them their names, the people who inhabited this region came to be referred to as the Getae or Dacians by the Greeks. Eventually, during the reign of the Roman emperors, the name Dacians became the accepted term. After the defeat of their king, Decebal, through the bravery of Nerva Trajan, this population was mostly eradicated, scattered like the four winds.[4] The entire region was brought under Roman occupation and transformed into a Roman province, divided, and given to Roman citizens. There were three parts: Dacia Ripensis, Dacia Mediterranea, and Dacia Alpestris. The first consisted of Hungary and Wallachia; Transylvania

---

[4] The Dacian population was not eradicated but mixed with Roman colonists from throughout the Empire. Over time, this assimilation led to the formation of the Romanian people.

was given the name "Mediterranea", and much of our Moldavia became "Dacia Alpestris," which was located between the Prut River and the Danube, and the lands bordering Wallachia. After the end of Roman rule, Moldavia was repeatedly invaded by various barbarian tribes such as the Sarmatians, Huns, and Goths. As a result, the Roman colonies were compelled to flee across the mountains to find refuge in the rugged terrain of Maramureș to escape the violence of these migratory populations. After several centuries of living there under local laws and native rulers, a time during which they were protected from the harshness of the surrounding regions, around the year of our Lord… because of overcrowding due to a large number of inhabitants, Dragoș, son of Bogdan, their leader, decided to cross over the mountains to the east, but only with a group of three hundred people, as though he were going hunting. On his way, he encountered a wild bison by chance, known as an "auroch" by the Moldavians. They followed it until they found themselves at the foot of the mountains. Once there, Molda, Dragoș's hunting dog, which he loved more than all the others, fiercely chased the wild animal, leading the bison to jump into the river. The auroch was killed on the spot with arrows, and the dog, which had followed it into the water, was engulfed by the swift currents. In her memory, Dragoș named that river "Moldova," and the place where all of this happened was named "Roman" after his nation. He also decided that his new coat of arms would depict an auroch. While exploring the neighboring areas, he stumbled upon fertile fields irrigated by rivers and fortified towns and forts, but they had been deserted by their inhabitants. He told his people about this discovery and asked them to occupy this very fertile land. The young Romans eagerly heeded the call of their ruler and rode together in large groups through the mountainous passes.

Overjoyed upon reaching their destination, they dismounted and proclaimed Dragoș, their discoverer, as the first prince of that settlement.[5] Thus, the land and Roman rule were once again in the hands of their rightful masters after a long time. Subsequently, the land lost its Roman and Dacian name and came to be recognized as "Moldova" by locals and foreigners alike, named after the river that flowed through it. However, the new name was not accepted by everyone; for example, the Turks, who frequently invaded this region due to their dominion over nearby European lands, initially referred to Moldavians *Ak Ulachs*. At the behest of his dying father Stephen, Bogdan submitted the country to their rule.[6] These people typically referred to their conquered territories by the name of their ruling leaders, which meant that Moldavians were known as *Bogdanli*. However, the old name was kept unchanged in the Tatar language. The neighbors on the other side, the Poles and the Russians, named this population *Volochs*, which meant "Italians" and the Wallachians were named *Munteni*, meaning people who live in mountain areas.

---

[5] The Principality of Moldavia was founded in 1359 with Bogdan I as its Prince.

[6] This refers to Bogdan cel Orb (the Blind), the son of Stephen the Great, who submitted to Ottoman suzerainty in 1514.

Chapter II
About the Location of Moldavia, Its Past and Present Borders, and the Local Climate

Moldavia stretches from 44°54' to 48°51' latitude. The estimation of its longitude is uncertain, however, in the opinion of most geographers, the western part of the country, which borders Transylvania, is placed at 45°39' longitude. The other extremity, which ends at a sharp angle at Alba Iulia, or as the local people call it, Cetatea Albă, is located at 53°22' as can be seen on the map.[7] Because the regions near Transylvania are mountainous, and the other parts, which extend to Bessarabia,[8] Polish Ukraine, and the Danube, are flat fields, the climate is not uniform. In the mountainous areas, the wind blows colder, but at the same time healthier; while in the lowlands, the wind is warmer but less beneficial for the health.

---

[7] see Cantemir's map, p. 238.

[8] In Cantemir's time Bessarabia referred only to the southern district between the Prut and Dniester Rivers. After the Russian occupation of the area in 1812, it came to refer to the region between the Prut and the Dniester.

All things considered, Moldavia has not experienced the ravages of many diseases, particularly when compared to the warmer regions; only occasionally, and rarely, do the plague and malaria strike this land. It has been proven through experience that the plague is not caused by miasma; I have observed that this illness sometimes enters our region through Poland, in which cases its impact is more devastating, and other times through ships from Egypt and Constantinople, which regularly dock in the commercial harbor of Galați. The type of plague in Moldavia is different from that in other parts of Europe. This disease is usually quite devastating and contagious. Those who suffer from it usually die in not more than three days. Very few people survive for seven days, and even fewer patients recover from the disease. This disease is highly contagious, and even though the population is not greatly afraid of it, the closest friends of those affected by the plague are afraid to be near them. Climate change, poor eating habits, or the natural lack of physical strength, prevent the inhabitants from reaching old age. Seventy-year-old people are a rare sight, and eighty-year-olds are very hard to find. Despite their relatively short lifespans, the Moldavians enjoy good health throughout their lives, free from illnesses that would significantly hinder their happiness. Thus, they can make the most of their time and live life to the fullest. The peasants are said to live longer than those of noble blood who lead an easy life full of pleasures. We seldom experience earthquakes that disturb the existence of almost everyone in the warmer regions, and no town or mountain has ever been destroyed or collapsed because of them.

Moldavia has not always had the same borders: sometimes they were wider, and other times narrower, depending on the evolution of the state. Ultimately, Stephen the Great established the boundaries as they are today. The Danube, the largest waterway of Europe, has always formed Moldavia's southern border, and beyond that lies its delta where it branches out and empties into the Black Sea near Chilia, the old Lycostomon, or, as some call it, Achillea. The Black Sea has traditionally formed the eastern border of the country, but the Turks forcefully took Bessarabia and Bender, resulting in the loss of those territories. The Prut River remained as the border, from its estuary to the village of Traian. From this point, it joins with the Botna River and continues in a straight line until it reaches the source of the Bicu River where it converges with the Dniester River, as depicted by the maps. In the northern and eastern parts, the Dniester or Tyras River, called Turla by the Turks, separates the Poles from the Tartars settled in Oceakov; the territories along the riverbanks, up until Hotin were formerly governed by Moldavia, and beyond that point, the region's borders followed a straight line leading to the Prut and Ceremuș rivers. Later, through the courage of Stephen the Great, the adjacent land that bordered Podolia all the way to the source of the Serafineț River was annexed to Moldavia. As a result, the Dniester, Serafineț, Colacin, and Ceremuș rivers merged to form the northern border, at the point where the county of Ruthenian Câmpulung is located. Moldavia's western border became more expansive than ever before. Before the era of Stephen the Great, the adjacent mountains belonged to the people of Transylvania. Therefore, the western borders of Moldavia were relatively narrow. Thanks to his bravery, Stephen repeatedly defeated the Hungarian king, Matthias, and repelled the Transylvanians, compelling them into agreements to prevent further conflicts that could endanger them.[9] According to these agreements, the entire mountain chain that separated

---

[9] The most famous victory of Stephen the Great over Matthias Corvinus came at the battle of Baia in 1467 when the Hungarian king had to make an ignominious retreat after being soundly defeated by Moldavian forces.

the two countries became a Moldavian territory, along with all of the land encompassing the tributaries of the Moldova River. As a result, they traced a boundary line starting from the headwaters of the Ceremuș River, which followed the path of the Suceava, Moldova, Bistrița, and Trotuș Rivers, all the way to the source of the Milcov River. This line became the permanent border between the two territories. The frontier with Wallachia, historically marked by Siret and Trotuș rivers, changed when Stephen the Great successfully added the region of Putna to Moldavia; thus, the Milcov and Siret rivers came to separate the two countries. The ultimate southern boundary was the Danube. Limited by these frontiers, the circumnavigation of Moldavia takes 237 hours of walking or 711 Italian miles,[10] an estimate that can easily be made by anyone who might want to consult the map attached to this study. Long ago, when Bessarabia was not yet occupied by Turkish and Tartar armies, the circumnavigation of Moldavia took up to 247 hours of walking or 822 miles. With regard to its neighbors, the country is bordered by Transylvania and Wallachia to the west, Poland to the north, and the Turks to the east. In order to maintain their independence, the population had to vigorously resist all of these neighboring foes. A reliable Polish historian claims about the Moldavians: "Their way of life does not differ much from the Italian one if we consider their nature, traditions, and language. They fought ruthlessly and valiantly, and no other people could match their glory and courage in warfare, despite the onslaughts that came at them from all directions. Despite being a small nation, surrounded by hostile neighbors, they have always defended themselves and fought in wars to secure a better future for themselves." He also

---

[10] An Italian mile was 1,834 meters.

added: "Their resilience was so formidable that they would be victorious even when fighting all of their neighboring foes at the same time. In fact, Stephen, who also ruled Dacia during the time of our forefathers, had defeated Bayezid the Turk, Matthias the Hungarian, and John Albert the Pole in a single summer, during a great war" (*Orichovius*, Annal 5, in the year 1552). Eventually, after falling under Turkish rule, the state never became involved in wars other than those against the Turks, and they came to share the same allies and foes as them. The only exception was the Nogai Tartars, whom the Turks had sheltered in Bessarabia, who continued to raid Moldavia repeatedly, even during times of peace. This was a major factor that contributed to the country's current state of poverty.

Chapter III
About the Waters of Moldavia

It would be hard to find another land as narrow as Moldavia, blessed with such abundant bodies of water, peculiarly placed there by nature itself. There are four large navigable rivers: the Danube, the Dniester, the Prut, and the Siret. Despite bordering only a small part of Moldavia, the Danube remains the most advantageous for the country's governance. Indeed, apart from the commercial vessels from various nations that bring their goods and dock in the harbor of Galați, the Moldavians also benefit from the opportunity to transport their own goods down the Prut, straight to Constantinople and other towns along the coast of the Black Sea. This allows them to earn considerable profits. There is no need for me to go into further detail about this river and the riches hidden in its depths because many have already done so in descriptions of Germany and Hungary, and they have covered all that is worth mentioning.

The Prut River, which was originally called Hierasus by Ptolemy, Gerasus by Ammianus, and Pyretus by the ancient Greeks, flows into the Danube. It has its source in Transylvania, in the Carpathian Mountains, which were known as the Carpathians of ancient times, and forms the border with Poland, dividing Moldavia into two parts. It has the purest and healthiest water that I have ever known, even though the sand that flows with it might give it a slightly murky appearance. If the water is poured into a glass jar, the sand will settle at the bottom, leaving behind clear water. While in Moldavia, I conducted an experiment and I found a way to weigh a hundred drams of this fluid. I discovered that this quantity is thirty drams lighter than the exact same amount of water taken from any other river.

The Siret is the only river that belongs entirely to Moldavia, flowing from the most remote areas bordering Poland, in a southward direction to the Danube, into which it flows in two places. This waterway is fairly wide and deep, but due to its surroundings, which consist mainly of forests and mountains, and because of the rifts that occasionally appear, it has not yet been opened to navigation for ships.

The Dniester River, called Tyras or Dinastris by Greek writers and the Turla by the Turks, flows south along the eastern side of the country. It is well-known to everyone so there's no need for me to say more about it. I would like to mention that this river was used by the Turks to transport their troops, supplies, and war materials from Constantinople, through the Black Sea, all the way up to Bender, and once even to Camenița, today as far as Hotin. Although its water seems clear, it is impure and very harmful to those who drink from it. This river flows into the Black Sea at Alba Iulia (Cetatea Albă).

Apart from the rivers mentioned above, some smaller waterways flow across Moldavia, such as:

The Bârlad River runs through the region of Tecuci, from east to west, and joins the Siret near the village of Șerbănești; I could not find the old name of this river;

The Suceava River was named for the city of Suceava, the former capital of the country;

The Moldova River is the one with the name I discussed previously (Chapter I);

The Bistrița River has its source in the Transylvanian Mountains and has such a fast and impetuous flow that it seizes and carries away anything that stands in its way, including the largest rocks over which it runs;

The Trotuș River is a waterway with a speed almost equal to the previously-mentioned river and has its source not far from the Bistrița;

The Prut River merges with the Ceremuș River, which marks the border between Moldavia and Poland, along with the Jijia River below;

The Răutul River flows into the Dniester River, which forms a delightfully enchanting island near Orhei, along with the Botna River, half of which is owned by the local Tartars of Bugeac.

Numerous small rivers run across the Moldavian territory. I will not forget to mention the more significant ones, whose names I managed to discover. The following rivers flow into the Siret: Bănilă, Molnița, Șomuzul Mare and Șomuzul Mic, Valea Neagră, Faraon, Răcătău, Gerul Sohului, Milcov, and Putna; the last two merge and become Sirețel, which means the Little Siret.

The waters of the Sucevița, Solca, and Solonț flow into the Suceava River and enhance its debit. The streams of Humor, Slatina, Rîșca, Neamț, Topolița, Valea Albă, and others flow into the Moldova River. The tiny river of Cracău flows into the Bistrița River. Into the Trotuș River flows the Tazlău Sărat and the other Tazlău, as well as the Oituz, Cașin, and Valea Rea rivers. Into the Bârlad River flow the waterways of Bîrlădeț, Sacovăț, Vilna, Rebricea, Vaslui, Vasluieț, Racova, Crasna, Lohan, Docolina, Hobîlna, Horiata, Smila, Tutova, Berheci, Zeletin, and Corod. The Black Ceremuș, White Ceremuș, and Putila waterways join to form the Ceremuș River. The Jijia River receives the waters of the Șubana, Sitna, Milet, Bahlui, Bahluieț, and Sîrca. The Colacin, Coțman, Cuciur (Ciuciur), Chiur, Bașeu, Corovia, Caminca, Căldărușa, Jijia, Gârla Mare, Delia, Valea

Mare, Valea Brătuleni, Moșna, Nirnova, Călmățui, Lăpușna, Strîmba, eastern and western Sărata, Tigheciu, Larga, and Elan waterways flow into the Hierasus or Prut River.

The Dniester River is fed by small Moldavian rivers, such as the Ciorna, Iachel, Bîcovăț, Iznovăț, Bîcu, and Serafineț, the mouth of which forms the easternmost point of Moldavia.

In Moldavia, the Răut River is fed by the waters of the Solonoț, Ciulucul-Mare, Ciulucul-Mic, and Ciuclucul Mijlociu, as well as the Dobrușa, Cula, and Cogîlnic streams. In Bessarabia, the Cahul, Salcea, and Ialpug Rivers flow into the Danube, and the Cogîlnic River flows into the Dniester.

Out of all the names mentioned above, only the Ialpug has consistently flowed. The others are more like ponds than flowing bodies of water. The Cogîlnic, for instance, had no natural springs, and only swells with autumn rains, becoming a true river at that time. Throughout the summer it remains dry and empty like a ditch, and, as a result, the cattle of the Bugeac Tartars often die from the lack of water.

Moldavia has no shortage of lakes either. Among the multitude, both natural and artificial, five are to be mentioned in particular:

Brateș Lake, which can be found between the Prut and Siret rivers, near the city of Galați, stretches about an Italian mile in width and two miles in length.[11] It does not have any natural sources but is sustained by the Prut River through a narrow and shallow brook called the Pruteț. This brook only carries water when the Prut River swells due to rain and precipitation; the rest of the time, it is just a dry brook, which sometimes gives the lake a strong odor. In the spring, the Danube not only pushes back the Prut River but also fills

---

[11] See note 10.

the whole lake with fresh water and an abundance of fish. This allows the locals to catch fish easily when the water recedes.

Orhei Lake, located near the city of the same name, was formed by Răut and Cula Rivers and is six miles in length and two miles in width. The size of the lake was extended by a terrace built by the ruler Vasile the Albanian[12] to prevent water from flowing out and to build mills that could generate an increase in earnings. The lake also contained a small island in the middle, planted with vines, which were once very famous, and various types of fruit trees.

Dorohoi Lake, named as such for the nearby town of the same name, located not far from the source of the Jijia River, is worthy to be mentioned for its multitude of fish.

Colacin Lake, on the border with Poland, is noteworthy, especially because the northern and southern sides were the sources of the Colacin and Serafineț streams, which mark the Moldavian border with Poland, between Dniester and Prut rivers.

The last and most well-known lake was Lake Ovidius, named by the locals Ovid's Lake, close to Akkerman, formerly Alba Iulia. Located in Bessarabia, it was illustrious, particularly for its name, because it was said that the legendary Roman poet Ovid was forced to live his life in exile there.[13] This lake connects to the Dniester River through a narrow brook near its mouth. However, due to the presence of numerous large swamps, a person could not cross its width on foot for nearly 2 Italian miles. A bridge of very ancient construction links the two shores, as I could deduce from its architecture; the sturdiness

---

[12] This refers to Moldavian Prince Vasile Lupu, of Albanian descent.

[13] See Adrian Rădulescu, *Ovid in Exile* (Las Vegas: Center for Romanian Studies, 2019)

of this architectural work and the size of the rocks used for its construction attest to its age.

All of the waters and ponds that I have described up to this point are full of particularly good fish. The creeks that flow down from the mountain peaks are home to delicious trout, salmon, and graylings, which are brought to the ruler's table daily, particularly during periods of fasting.

Moldavia doesn't have any thermal, acidulated, or mineral waters, or at least they have not been discovered thus far. However, the water of the Prut River is said to have medicinal properties that can cure various illnesses.

Chapter IV
About the Counties and Towns of Moldavia

Moldavia was once comprised of three regions — Lower Moldavia, Upper Moldavia, and Bessarabia — which included a total of 23 counties. However, as time passed, this changed. Bessarabia came under Turkish domination due to the betrayal of a ruler named Aron, who gave away Tighina and two other counties to them. As a consequence, the current rulers were left with only 19 counties, some of which are not even complete.

Lower Moldavia, called by the locals "the lower country," is comprised of 12 smaller counties, which were known as lands (*ținuturi*). In the middle of this region stands:

1. IAȘI COUNTY. The city of Iași, the capital of Moldavia, is located along the Bahlui River, four miles from its confluence with the Prut River. It was chosen by Stephen the Great as the new center of his reign after moving it from Suceava, to better protect his domain from attacks by the Turks and the Tartars, from the heart of the country. He decided to move the center of his reign here because of its more strategic location closer to the borders, which would make it harder for invaders to attack. Before his court arrived, Iași was an insignificant village, with only three or four cottages and a mill. This was the property of an old miller named Ioan [John], known by the nickname Iași. The ruler wished to preserve this name for the city that he planned to establish. He began by building a church dedicated

to Saint Nicholas,[14] which later became a cathedral. After that, he proceeded to build large houses for himself and his noblemen. The ruler, Radu, surrounded Iași with walls, while other rulers decorated it and erected public buildings, resulting in the city having more than 40 churches, some made of brick, others made of wood, with the majority being well-built. Fifty years ago, at the census, 12,000 individual homes were counted, but since then, due to frequent fires, outbreaks of plague, and attacks by the Tartars and the Poles, this city has become so desolate that barely a third of it remained untouched. In addition to the court, which collects taxes for the whole country, the residence of the Metropolitan of Moldavia is located here, although he is referred to as the "Metropolitan of Suceava," after the former capital, and not "of Iași." The town of Iași had only one archpriest of its own, about whom we shall speak more later. This county is bordered to the south by

2. CÂRLIGĂTURA COUNTY, which has little of note except for Târgul Frumos, the etymology of which means beautiful market, located 8 hours from Iași on the way to Suceava, also situated along the Bahlui River. This town should not be under-appreciated, as it has a stone palace belonging to the prince, over which presides a certain governor, called a *pârcălab* (meaning "commander"). Further on, to the west stretches

3. ROMAN COUNTY, the first region populated by Roman colonies after they returned from Transylvania following the invasion of Bathie (Batu-han) and renamed it with its former name. The town of Roman, known as Forum Romanorum, as Bonfinius writes, is located at the confluence of the Moldova and Siret Rivers. It is an archiepiscopal center and governed by two commanders (pâcălabi) appointed by the prince. Many believe this was the first settlement to

---

[14] Church of St. Nicholas in Iași.

be founded when our ancestors returned. But this theory is not accepted by everyone for, not far from there, on the southern shore of the Siret River, another place, called Smedorova, shows evidence that it was the first town settled, and that it used to be much bigger. What is certain is that this town was rebuilt long after the era of Stephen the Great, and restored to its former glory. However, after several years, it was abandoned once again for unknown reasons by Peter, called Rareş,[15] who ordered the inhabitants to relocate to the town of Roman. Toward the east, below Iaşi and Cârligătură counties, is located

4. VASLUI COUNTY. In this region, located at the confluence of the Vaslui and Bîrlad rivers and situated 12 hours away from Iaşi on the road to the Danube, lies the town of Vaslui. It was once the center of the principality, as evidenced by the royal residences of former princes that can still be seen there. The commander of Vaslui was entrusted with its leadership after the capital was moved to Iaşi. To the south, extends in length

5. TUTOVA COUNTY, which took its name from the Tutova River that appeared to slice it in two. The most important town in this region is Bârlad, located on the river with the same name, formerly a significant town in size, but currently left forgotten and stripped of all of its fineries. This is the residence of the commander of Lower Moldavia, known as the "vornic" of Lower Moldavia. However, due to his obligation to always follow his superiors, he is replaced by two smaller "vornici." One Italian mile downstream, on

---

[15]Petru Rareş (1527-1538; 1541-1546), an illegitimate son of Stephen the Great, spent many years in exile at the Polish court. He came to the throne with the support of the Moldavian boyars in 1527. During his two reigns, he tried to extend his rule over Transylvania and he sought to restore the independence of Moldavia by playing the neighboring great powers off against each other.

the same shore, lie the ruins of a very old citadel, known as "The Ground Citadel." None of the foundations or any remaining artifacts have ever been found that would allow us to determine anything conclusive about its founders. Only a few walls on the ground can be seen, leading me to believe they were built long ago by the residents to defend against Tartar attacks.

6. THE LAND OF TECUCI borders Bârlad to the west; it is fairly large, but has little worth mentioning apart from the town of Tecuci on the Bârlad River. It's located 8 hours between Bârlad and Galați. This ugly little town without any walls is the place where two commanders responsible for the administration of the region were once stationed. To the west of it, on the shores of the Siret River, there is

7. THE LAND OF PUTNA, which appeared to be named for the Putna River. Within this region lies Focșani, a little town along the Milcov River, located at the border with Wallachia. The leader of Wallachia was responsible for the matters of that land. The town of Adjud, located upstream on the Siret River, is too insignificant to be discussed. At the foot of the Vrancea Mountains, not far from Mira, stands the memorial monastery to the ruler Constantine Cantemir's[16] humbleness and faithfulness. Close by were the ruins of an ancient citadel, but I could not find any evidence of the period it was built in or its founders. This place is known by the locals as "Crăciuna." On the other shore of the Siret River, between the Siret, Danube, and Prut Rivers, standing in the middle is

---

[16] Constantine Cantemir was of yeoman origin and almost illiterate (he knew only how to sign his name). The boyars brought Constantine Cantemir to the throne because they thought he could be easily manipulated. To their dismay, he proved to be an authoritarian ruler, executing two of the most important boyars in the country, Velicico Costin and his brother, the famous chronicler, Miron Costin, the most profound political and historical thinker of old Romanian literature.

8. THE CORVULUI LAND. Its name was taken from the Covurlui Creek, which despite being located 8 hours away, was always dry and seldom did it fill with water. Of note in the area is the town of Galați, deservedly remembered not only for the beauty of its buildings and size but also for being the most famous harbor on the entire Danube. Twice or three times a year, ships, not only from the surrounding Black Sea coast but also from the Crimean Peninsula, Trapezunt, Sinope, Constantinople, Egypt, and even Bessarabia, would dock in Galați. The ships would return loaded with Moldavian wood, such as oak, eglantine, and pine, as well as honey, wax, salt, butter, saltpeter, and oats, which brought significant earnings to all the inhabitants of Moldavia. Not far from here, to the east of the Siret River's springs, lie the ruins of an ancient citadel, known as Gherghina by the locals. It is believed to have been established during Trajan's reign, as evidenced by coins and a piece of marble with this inscription:

IMP. CAESARI. DIV. FILIO. NERVAE. TRAIANO.
AUGUSTO. GERM. DACICO. PONT. MAX. FEL. B.DICT.

XVI. IMP. VI. CONS. VII. P. P.
CALPURNIO. PUBLJO. MARCO. C.AURELIO RUFO

Upstream on the Prut River, we find:

9. THE LAND OF FĂLCIU in which the town of Fălcii was located. This is not an average town you see along the Prut. Through my research, I discovered traces of an ancient citadel nearby, which showed evidence that this area was once inhabited by the Taifs. In a handwritten copy of the Histories of Herodotus, I came across a passage stating the Taif people, a tribe of warriors, lived by the Prut River, three days' journey from the course of the Istru, and had built

a magnificent citadel. However, despite scouring the fields, no remnants of the citadel were found. Thus, I dispatched experts from the area to search the neighboring woods for evidence that could help us pinpoint the precise location of the stronghold. Upon their return, they told me they had found the foundations of walls and towers made of burnt brick in the thick woods on the western side. These structures extended up to five Italian miles towards the river. Furthermore, they said that even if these structures could not be observed on the surface of the surrounding fields, they had an oblong (elliptical) shape. Besides that, the current name of this land has strengthened my belief that "Fălcii" is a corrupted form of the word "Taiphalia" given the similarity between them. Located in the middle of this region lays Huşi, a little townlet that serves as an episcopal center, but is otherwise unremarkable, except for the heroic battle fought there in 1711. During that battle, Peter the Great, Tsar of Russia, valiantly defended against continuous attacks by the Turks for four days with only a small army. Not far from this Huşi, there's a moderately-sized, man-made mound, named by the Tartars "Han Tepesi," which meant "the mound of the khan." The locals call it "the mound of Răbîi." There are different opinions about its origin. Some believe a khan of the Tartars was defeated and killed there by the Moldavian army, and his people built it in his memory; others believe a Scythian queen named Rabie, led her army against the Scythians living in Moldavia but died and was been buried in that spot by her people. I hesitate to determine what is true and what is not in all this darkness of the story. On the northern side of this region there is

10. THE LAND OF LĂPUŞNA. This region had once included the town of Tighina, also known as Bender by the Turks. It was once a highly fortified citadel, and the Turks added more fortified structures on the Dniester River. Recently, it served as a refuge for the

king of Sweden after his defeat at Poltava. Despite the Turks' persistent siege, they were unable to take the citadel by force. Eventually, they succeeded through deception and betrayal by the ruler Aron, whom the Moldavians called "The Tyrant." After being removed from power by the boyars due to his cruel and oppressive treatment of the Moldavian population, he fled to the Turkish Sultan and promised to give the town of Tighina, along with 12 villages, to their army, as they had repeatedly requested if he were to be restored to power. Tempted by this gift, the Sultan reinstated him as ruler of Moldavia. As a token of appreciation for his support, he received the strongest citadel in the entire country, which offered the best defensive barrier against the Poles and the Tartars.

As a result, the most important fortress in the region is Lăpușna, situated along the river of the same name. The ruler appointed two commanders to oversee the affairs of the land. Apart from it, on the Bîcu watercourse, there is Chișinău, a small town, but this town is insignificant. Not far from this location, there is a row of giant rocks, arranged in such a straight line that appears they were placed like this by people. What made me doubt this idea was both the size of the rocks and the vast distance they cover. Some of them are square-shaped measuring three or four *cot* units[17] and the whole row stretched beyond the stream of Dniester, up to the Crimea. In the local language, this was called "Bîcu's dock" and the naive peasants believed this was the devil's work, who had sworn to obstruct the Bîcu River's flow. Several rulers attempted to dam this river which flows through the mountains, in order to create a lake for the nearby

---

[17]*Author's Note:* Cot (tr. Elbow) is an old unit of measurement for length equal to 0.664 meters (in Muntenia) or 0.637 meters (in Moldova), representing the distance from the elbow to the wrist.

commercial areas. However, they have never been successful. Above this, bordering the Dniester River, there is

11. THE LAND OF ORHEI. This region is named for the town of Orhei, located on the course of Răut. Although not so big, it's remarkable in its own way for the rich resources essential for human existence. The Orhei Lake lies close to the burg on the eastern side. It has a wonderful island, which I talked about previously and more extensively in Chapter III.[18] It provided the locals with abundant sources of food. The last region along the shores of the Dniester is

12. THE LAND OF SOROCA. This is the most significant fortress is Soroca, formerly known as Alchionia.[19] It's located along the Dniester River in a field, near some hills. Despite its small size, it was built during a period when fortifications were of utmost importance and it was made to endure and not collapse. Its walls are square-shaped, very strong, fortified with very tall towers, and made from flint from the surrounding hills. The lack of water and wood in the northern parts of the region made cultivation almost impossible, resulting in the only desert to be found in Moldavia, although it is not particularly large. For this reason, the region was noted more for its wilderness in more precise geographical books. Following the loss of Tighina, Soroca became a crucial stronghold against the Poles, and two army generals were appointed to defend the fortress.

Upper Moldavia, named by the locals "The Upper Country," contains seven smaller lands.

---

[18] *Author's Note:* On the southern shore of the lake, amidst the surrounding planted forests, traces of an old fortress known as Old Orhei can be seen. Its location suggests that it may have been the same as the ancient Dacian Petrodava.

[19] *Author's Note:* I was unable to determine how the Moldavian historian, Nicolae Costin, discovered it was previously called Olchionia. However, in the ancient description of Dacia, it was situated in the same location as Carsidava once was.

1. THE LAND OF HOTIN stretches along the Dniester's course, north of Soroca. The fortress of Hotin, located on the Dniester River before Camenița, is considered to be one of the greatest structures of Moldavia.[20] In the past, it was protected by high barriers and deep trenches on the southern side, and on the eastern side by nature itself through the steep shore and rocky ravines of the Dniester. However, in the last war with the Russians, the Turks uncovered the ancient walls of the fortress that they had conquered in 1712. On the opposite side, they fortified it with strong and modern structures, enlarging it by more than half. Today, it is considered the most beautiful and well-fortified of all the Moldavian fortresses. During the time it was under Moldavian rule, it was carefully entrusted to a certain headman. After being invaded by the Turks, it was placed under the rule of a Turkish pasha, contrary to the agreements made with the Poles, who strongly opposed the Turkish garrisons[21] in Moldavian fortresses. To the south follows

2. THE LAND OF DOROHOI, containing the town of Dorohoi, a relatively unimportant settlement located near the springs of the Jijia River. This was the home of the Upper Country's governor, who was responsible for the leadership of this entire territory. Due to his court duties, he was unable to attend to the affairs of his region, thus he appointed two smaller governors for this purpose. The town of Ștefănești, situated on the Prut River, was said to have a harbor for boats and a repository of supplies for the Hotin garrison, which had

---

[20] *Author's Note:* I believe this is Triphulum of old Dacia or Arcobodava, if Clepidava and Camenița are one and the same, according to the opinion of Mattheus Praetorius, even though the latter is located on the southern banks of the Dneister River, not the northern one.

[21] *Author's Note:* This was the damage from which Moldavia suffered after its missfortune.

been built by the Turks after they cleared up the river. Down from there is located

3. THE LAND OF HÎRLĂU. The town of Hîrlău was not particularly famous and was governed by a certain "pârcălab" (or commander). Cotnar is a borough famous for its exceptional vineyards, which could be easily distinguished from other types. The management of these vineyards was entrusted to a *Great Paharnic* responsible for pouring wine into the ruler's glass during important feasts. In this location, the Catholic residents had churches made of stone, with beautiful architecture. Botoșani is a town that, together with the neighboring areas, was favored by the ruler's wife. Their income was collected by a pantry clerk, chosen to take care of this task. All these regions are brought together in harmony by

4. THE LAND OF CERNĂUȚI, along the Polish border. Cernăuți is the most significant town in this region and it's located on the northern shore of the Prut River. Its governance was assigned to the great governor known as the "Spătar." Near the village of Cozmin, on the watercourse of the Ciur River, not far from the place it merges with the Prut River's waters, lie the ruins of a very old fortress. Despite my persistent and diligent research, I was unable to discover anything about its founders. From the western shore of the Siret River, we reach

5. THE LAND OF SUCEAVA. Several towns are noteworthy in this county. Suceava was once the capital of Moldavia, the ruler's seat, and the residence of the Metropolitan, but currently, it is mostly in ruin. Located on a gentle hill on the banks of the Suceava River, its namesake, it is surrounded by walls and very deep grooves.[22] The city under the fortress spread over the hill's plateau. Apart from the

---

[22]*Author's Note:* According to its location and the similarity in names, I believe that it could be Sandava of ancient Dacia.

homes of the ruler and the noblemen, there were forty stone churches, and many more made of wood, as well as 16,000 individual houses, that were all demolished after the ruler decided to move his seat to Iași. Currently, its governance is the responsibility of the *hatman*, the supreme commander of the army. Another important town is Rădăuți, which is an episcopal center close to Suceava, on the same river and the Siret waterway, located at the spot where the river changes course to the south.

6. THE LAND OF NEAMȚ is in immediate proximity and covers a significantly large area between the Moldavia and Bistrița Rivers. The fortress of Neamț, located on the river with the same name, was built on a very high mountain and fortified by nature itself, and it appeared to have never been touched by enemy attacks. Even though it was attacked several times, it was only conquered twice, first by the Turks under the command of Suleiman, and recently by John Sobieski, the king of Poland. It would not have been conquered if the few Moldavians guarding it had not surrendered because of hunger after a couple of days of siege. It once had double walls and only one gate allowed traffic. After the exterior wall was destroyed by the Turks, the Moldavians were left only with the interior one. Before Moldavia was subdued by the Turks, every time a war broke out, the rulers would send their children and riches to be sheltered in this resilient fortress. Even now, when the locals are attacked by the neighbors, they find safety here. For this purpose, the rulers once built large houses, which can be seen there today, although not as well-preserved as they should be. Directly across, on the Bistrița River, lies the town of Piatra. The list ends with:

7. THE LAND OF BACĂU, governed by a *vornic*. His residence was in the town of Bacău, on an island in the Bistrița River, famous for the wealth brought by business with fruits and produce. In addition, there is a bishop of the Western Church, known as the Bishop

of Bacău. Below the mountainous regions, there were many people in servitude to Moldavians. They called themselves Catholics by religion and nation. After defeating King Matthiaș of Hungary, Stephen the Great relocated these people from that country and gave them to the boyars. Their most important village is Cantemirești in the Land of Roman, also known as named Faraoani. It encompasses over 200 Catholic families who practice their faith in a very old stone church. Ocna and Trotuș, located on the banks of the Trotuș River, are not very important towns for anything other than the famous salt mines found nearby. This area serves as the largest crossing point between Moldavia and Transylvania.

Bessarabia was once the third region of Moldavia, and is mostly flat land, without mountains or forests, and with only one river, the Ialpug River, that has a consistent flow throughout the year. It does not have any springs or smaller rivers, a result of the residents digging deep wells to combat the lack of water. Instead of wood, they use sun-dried cattle manure to heat their homes. This region was subjugated by the Turks before the rest of the country and is no longer under Moldavian rule. Despite this, today the towns and villages are full of Christian Moldavians who suffer under the oppression of the two pagan oppressors, the Tartars and the Turks, both under the command of a *seraschier*.[23] The regions of Bessarabia consist of four main territories: Buceag, Akkerman, Chilia, and Izmail.

In the middle of them, there is:

1. BUCEAG,[24] a settlement of the Nogaic Tartars, which now some call the Buceag Tartars, and others call Bielograd Tartars (of

---

[23] Army Commander and Minister of War in the Ottoman Empire.

[24] *Author's Note:* In the Tartar language, the word for "angle" referred to the region between the Danube and Dniester rivers because it extended sharply toward the Black Sea, forming a distinct angle at its end. This geographical feature resembled

the White Fortress). Around 976, the year of Hegira, or year 1568 from the birth of our Lord, the Crimea Khan was ordered by Selim the Second to link the Don and Volga rivers. However, more than thirty families of Nogaic Tartars, who had previously been obedient to Russian rule, rejected this idea and migrated to Crimea. Because of the limited capacity of the Chersones to accommodate all of them, the Nogaic Tartars were given settlements in Buceag. Over time, as other Tartar families joined them, their population grew so much that it was almost as numerous as other Scythian hoards. They divided themselves into two tribes, "Orac Ougly" and "Orumbet Ougly," and tried as much as possible to preserve their bloodline pure. By custom, they live their lives on the plains, without building towns, except for the town of Căuşani, located on the Botna River, which extends over a small surface of the land. Once, however, this region had some very nice towns, as evidenced by the ruins of an ancient fortress on the shore of the Dniester River, currently called Tatarpunar, meaning "the Tartars' well." It is located on a very high rock, from which a clear spring flows at its foot. No inscriptions or traces of the fortress's builder have been found to this day. Similarly, on the Ialpug

---

the ancient Besi name that was used by the region's early geographers and historians. It has been suggested that the name "Bessarabia" may have originated from the ancient tribes of the Besi and Getae. Ovid, in his lament "How pathetic it is to live among the Besi and Getae," makes reference to these peoples. Ptolemy's Geography mentions the Peucins and Bastarns in the region of Upper Dacia, and some scholars, including Mattheus Praetor in Book II, Chapter 7, believed that the Bastarns and the Besis were one and the same. Praetor writes: "There are some who believe that the Bastarns are exactly the same nation that were once called Besi, named today Basarabi, meaning the residents of Bessarabia."

River, not far from its source, there are the remnants of an old fortress, commonly known as Tint[25]. After its decline, Stephen the Great rebuilt it. Later, however, the Turks burned it to the ground, and now only the location of the fortress can be seen. From its ruins, they built another fortress, in front of the old one, which still stands to this day and is known as Tobac. It is located on the coast of the Black Sea, perhaps where the ancient Aepolium once stood.

2. THE LAND OF AKKERMAN. Here lies the Akkerman, known by the locals as "The White Fortress," by the ancient Romans as Alba Iulia,[26] by the Greeks as Moncastron, and by the Polish as Bielograd. It's a large and strong citadel, located right along the Black Sea. When it was under the rule of Moldavia, it was managed by the *Great Logofăt*. Currently, it's administered by the Turkish commander of the Janissaries. Long ago, it became famous thanks to Saint John the New who became a martyr at the hands of the Turkish Emperor. His miraculous relics, along with the whole treasury and wealth of the rulers, were taken from Moldavia by John Sobieski, the King of Poland. Despite his claims of fighting for the Church and Jesus Christ, he used the financial support of the Pope to carry out this act.

Downstream, on the shores of the Danube lies:

---

[25] *Author's Note:* The location of the Tint fortress appears to be close to the Hărmănești village, if only the Hărmănești in question was not the one in Tatarbunar that was previously discussed.

[26] *Author's Note:* According to Bonfinius Decad. I, libr. I, page 23, Hungary not only had this Alba (Regia) but also a Greek one on the Taurin River, as well as Alba Iulia in Dacia, which fortunately retained the name of the ancestors.

3. THE LAND OF CHILIA. The most important fortress in the region is Chilia,[27] once called Lycostomon. It is located at the north-

---

[27] *Author's Note:* Known by the Moldavians and the Turks as "Chili", by the newer Greeks as Lycostomon" (badly translated by some, in my opinion, as „Lytrostomon" or "Lythostroton"), see Leuncl. (Pandect. 146). Bonfinius and others believed this was Achilea. Stanislaus Sarnicius tentatively identified it as Tomis, the fortress where Ovidius Naso was exiled. Among the various opinions of so many authors, I couldn't decide which one was true. However, based on my average knowledge of those places, I would say it without hesitation. If there had ever existed a Tomis town, which had been famous for the exile of Ovid, it surely couldn't be the one that, according to the old Mysia's map, was placed in the middle of the region, on the watercourse of Naxos. Historians who mentioned that city could easily prove the contrary, and even Ovid himself declared that he had been living in exile on Sarmatian ground: "Ne mea Sarmaticum contegat ossa solum" (The Sarmatian ground shall not cover my bones).Therefore, Tomis was also a city of Sarmația. The same poet described the rivers of this region, reffering to the Dniester and Dneiper, which were far away from Naxos, as anyone could see. This was also confirmed by the poet's written-in-stone epitaph, which was discovered by Stanislaus Sarnicius. However, he said that one Polish nobleman found and read in the village of Isac (misspelled Asac) a stone with this inscription:

> Hic situs est vates, quem diri Caesaris ira
>
> Augusti patria cedere iussit humo.
>
> Saepe miser voluit patriis occumbere terries,
>
> Sed trustera; hunc ili fata dedere locum.

The same poet expressed his sadness about living among the Besi and Getae. It was evident that he had been exiled to Sarmația, near the Dniester or Dneiper rivers where Tomis was located. To learn more about this, we should look at the ancient historians. Sozomen wrote in his Ecclesiastical History, Book 6, Chapter 20, about the Scythian settlements. He mentioned that this nation had many towns, villages, and forts, and that the most important one was Tomis, a wealthy and grand city located near the sea. When someone arrived by boat on the Black Sea, there was a

ern mouth of the Danube, and it was named by the Greek sailors because it appeared to merge with the waves, resembling a wolf's throat. The fortress is not very large, but the commercial dock is famous, as it has been visited by various types of ships, not only from the nearby maritime fortress but also from distant ones, such as Egyptian, Venetian, Ragusan vessels which usually brought wax and raw cowhide. Its residents are not only Turks but also Jews, Christians, Armenians, and people of other nationalities, which are overseen by a supervisor known colloquially as a "nazir." During the reign of Suleiman, it was set on fire by the Moldavians and it has not regained its former glory since then. On the eastern bank of the Danube River lies:

4. THE LAND OF ISMAIL. Important locations from this region include the town of Ismail, formerly called "Smil" by the Moldavians, which contains a strong fortress reinforced by the Turkish army with a "muteweli." The town of Cartal is situated at the point where the Danube merges with the Ialpug, in front of the small fortress

---

long-standing tradition that a bishop would be the leader of the Church for the entire nation. During the time of Valentinian and Valens, when Valens visited Tomis, the town was being managed by Britannio. After the king had to return to the Church, the bishop, who was unwilling to meet him and was tainted by the Aryan heresy, left the king alone. This made the king angry, and he exiled Britannio. However, the Scythians were deeply upset about the bishop's banishment, and Valens was worried that this could cause a rebellion. The Scythians were needed and brave, as they were able to fend off the barbarian attacks in the region, making them strategically important for the Roman Empire. After a time, Valens allowed Britannio to return, as he did not want to start a revolution. The bishop was well-respected among the Scythians for his holiness, and his actions helped to defeat the king's plans. All of this was written by Sozomen.

About the Counties and Towns of Moldavia

called Isaccea. Over there, in 1711, during the Turkish-Russian war, a bridge was built across the Danube to move armies into Moldavia. For protection, they appointed a *dizdar*, who had a similar role to a commander. Renii (as the Moldavians called it) or Timarova (as the Turks called it) was another important fortress located near the confluence of the Prut and Danube rivers. Although under Turkish rule, no Turks could be seen. The garrison was composed of Moldavian Christians, with a commander called *beşli agasi*, led by Silistra's pasha who had the rank of a *seraskier*.

These are about all Moldavian fortresses and towns. They were provided with means for freedom and development, but tyranny, unfairness, and hostility toward developing states stole it away from them. Neither ancient nor modern historians could remember the founders of these locations and no inscriptions or monuments have been discovered that might provide any indications about the period of their inception or the nation responsible for their founding. Apart from the occasional scratches on walls left by later rulers who rebuilt them, no records or clues remain about their origins. Only Suceava had seven towers carved in a large stone, each topped by an imperial crown held by two lions. At the base of each tower, a stone band with two scaly fish can be seen, their heads down and their tails up, and an auroch's head beneath them. Between the horns of the auroch is a six-pointed star. As the auroch's head became the emblem of Moldavia only after the second establishment of the Romans, which I discussed in Chapter I, this stone sculpture seemed to be a testament to the restoration of Suceava's walls rather than their original construction. In addition, all of our nation's historians agree that when the Moldavians returned from Maramureş to their homeland they found strong and abandoned fortresses. This suggests their foundation could be traced to a much earlier period. The construction of most fortresses' walls proves that there were no signs of other architecture than the Roman one, except for the fortresses that I mentioned earlier, which were built to avoid the Tartar attacks and are more recent buildings. Most importantly, the accounts of the most esteemed Roman historians, provided convincing evidence that the major colonies of the Roman residents were established in Dacia by Emperor Trajan, and even though his successor Hadrian considered abandoning Dacia due to the fear of exposing them to extermination, he ultimately decided against it. However, he did leave many of his provinces on the Eastern side under the rule of the Barbarians. To all of these, there is also the eternal testimony of "The Trajan's Emperor Wave," which still bears the name of its creator. I have often wondered why this remarkable monument is not mentioned by ancient or more recent historians. As someone who has seen it myself, I can attest this fortification started at Petrovaradin in Hungary with a double ditch and descended to the Dermakapu Mountains (Iron Gate). From here it continued through Wallachia and Moldavia with a simple groove, crossed the Prut River in the village of Trajan and the Botna watercourse near the town of Căușani. It covered the entire Tartar land (Tartaria) and ended at the Don River. It still was as deep as 12 *coți*, from which we can deduce that at the time of construction, it had been almost twice as wide and deep, and furthermore, it had been an excellent fortification against foreign attacks. This being said, some claims[28] cannot be accepted, especially those saying that

---

[28] *Author's Note:* According to Bielski, on page 239, the Piecinicov and Polovcov nations were actually Lithuanians who came from the direction of the Cimmerian Bosporus and established friendly relations with the Genoese, who were in control

the Moldavian fortresses were built by the Genoese. The Roman soldiers who lived in the garrison all the time, could not survive without fortresses and shelters. However, it's difficult to imagine that the Genoese, who settled near the Black Sea for trade, would want to infiltrate Moldavia and build fortresses in areas better suited to agriculture than trade. If only someone had considered that they were built by the ancient Dacians during the reign of King Decebal, then it would have been clear that they were in a prosperous state before being occupied by the Romans and used as settlements for their colonies. Personally, I would not argue against such a notion.

---

of Chersonesos. Bielski also believes that these same Genoese, along with the Moldavians and Bessarabians, were responsible for building fortresses such as Mancob, Kerkel, Krym, Azov, Kafa, Achillea, Moncastron, Tyrgavisca, and others.

Chapter V
About the Mountains and Minerals of Moldavia

Along its western side, where Moldavia borders Transylvania and Wallachia, it is surrounded almost everywhere by high mountains. Because of this, the country was called "Mountainous Dacia" by the Romans. The Eastern side is characterized by fertile fields. The hills are naturally endowed with fruit trees, orchids, and other plants that would require special cultivation elsewhere, and the crystal-clear creeks cascading down the mountains produce a delightful murmur, turning the whole scenery into an indescribably beautiful garden. In turn, the fields plentifully provide the crops for which the cold mountainous air did not accord proper conditions for them to grow.

The most famous mountain is Ceahlău. If it had been recounted in the ancient legends, it certainly would not have been less famous than the Olympus, Pindus, or Pelias mountains. It is located in the land of Neamț, not far from the springs of Tazlău. Its slopes are covered in snow year-round, which does not melt with the change of seasons, but its peak is never snowy, as it rises far above the snowy clouds. From its peak, which rises in height like a tower, a brook with very clear water flows downhill, roaring and tumbling through the rocks in its path, until it merges with the Tazlău River. At the center of the area, there is an ancient statue, standing about three meters high, depicting an old lady surrounded by, if I am not mistaken, 20 sheep. The statue depicts an inexhaustible spring flowing from the genital organs of the sheep. It is, of course, hard to say if nature created this fantasy over time, or if the skilled hand of an artist forged it. The statue is not set on any pedestal, but while the rest of its body is one with the stone, the womb, and the torso are free. Even if we were to suppose that the cracks had been repaired with some kind of plaster, which I admit is a possibility given that many ancient works have been lost to the ravages of time, it is difficult to imagine how a duct could have been carved through the statue's leg to the particular area where the spring flows. There are no visible signs of any springs or water sources in the vicinity. It likely served as some kind of pagan idol, worshipped by acolytes who used natural or magical means to elicit wonder and awe from a gullible crowd, fostering a belief in the divine.

In fact, due to the height of the mountain, it is not surprising that, on cloudless days when the sun sets in the west, the fortress of Akkerman, located 60 hours away, could be seen clearly in its entirety, as if it were nearby. This is a phenomenon I haven't observed on any other summit, even the most famous ones. On the surrounding hills, there are visible traces of horses, dogs, and even wings, etched on the cliffs, as if a grand army of riders had passed along those paths. The locals tell many stories of them, but it's up to the naturalist to ascertain what is true.

There is another mountain range, commonly known as Ineu, located on the northern side near the Ceremuș River, where the borders of Moldavia, Poland, and Transylvania meet. Its height cannot be compared to Ceahlău, but it is no less impressive, as it also has a unique natural peculiarity not found anywhere else. The locals collect dew from plant leaves after sunrise, and, when put into a vessel, very good butter floats to the top, which does not differ from regular butter in smell, color, or taste. However, this does not happen throughout the year, only in March, April, and May, while during the other months, regardless of whether the months are wetter or drier. The nutritious value of that butter is so great that, if the sheep are taken up the mountains at that exact time, in a matter of a few days, they became overly fat. Shepherds, who knew of this phenomenon, kept their herds at the foot of the mountains during those months.

Our mountains do not lack the riches typical of mountainous regions, such as mineral deposits. In ancient times, the modest living conditions of the rulers and the absence of miners prevented them from exploiting these resources. Nowadays, the Moldavians are hindered by the greedy Turks and the fear that searching for such riches could cause them to lose their entire land, along with all their work and its benefits. Nevertheless, the proof of the existence of these underground riches can be found in the creeks that flowed at their base. The narrow riverbeds would often swell due to melting snow or rain, causing the water to overflow. When the waters receded, the brooks left behind sand that contained grains of the purest gold. The gypsies collected this sand and separated the impurities to obtain so much gold they could pay to the prince's wife a yearly tribute of four gold pots, worth 1,600 drachmas. In the land of Hotin, not far from the fortress itself, on the shore of Dniester River, there were natural iron deposits so large and round they could be used as cannon balls without any further processing. However, the iron itself was of low quality and, if it was not melted, it was completely useless. When Hotin was not considered a point of interest, the iron was transported to

Camenița, and it always seemed incredible to me that the Turks would have allowed the Poles to purchase what they needed for war at the expense of the Turks.

In the land of Bacău, near Trotuș, there are major salt deposits, which the locals call *ocne*. The salt here doesn't need to be refined: if the soil, up to half a meter to a meter deep, is removed, pure salt can be obtained, as clear as crystal or porphyry and devoid of any impurities. These *ocne* never seem to run out of salt, even if hundreds of people dig them up every day. Whenever a salt block was removed, pillars made of this crystal would be left behind, supporting the whole arch and ground, allowing new veins of salt to form. By doing so, within twenty years or so, the galleries created in this way would be filled with salt again, leaving no trace of ever being emptied. Sometimes miners found fish encrusted in salt blocks, which did not differ from those caught in the neighboring waters.

Salt deposits could be found in other places as well, but the rulers banned their exploitation, to prevent price drops and oversupply of this valuable resource, because the salt mines in work were sufficient to meet everyone's needs. There are entire mountains in Moldavia that, once their outer layer of earth was removed, appear to be made entirely of glass. From them, considerable wealth flows into the treasury of the prince and the entire nation, because, apart from the local population, the residents of Buceag and Crimea, and even those of distant countries, export salt from here with their ships.

Saltpeter can be found almost everywhere because nearly every field in Moldavia has black soil, which is rich in this resource.

At Tazlău-Sărat, not far from the village of Moinești, in the region of Bacău, tar or bitumen combined with water bubbles to the surface from a spring, which the peasants use to grease the wheels of their carts. The residents call it *păcură* and they say it could be better used in normal households if they could separate the water from it, as it is a better lamp fuel than the fuels obtained from trees.

Chapter VI
About the Fields and Forests of Moldavia

The fields of Moldavia, frequently mentioned for their fertility by both ancient and modern historians, greatly surpassed the riches of the mountains I described previously. Located in the middle of several other countries, separated from Moldavia by mountains and rivers, they can sustain the entire population even if left uncultivated. Crops that cannot grow in mountainous regions because of harsh conditions, such as storms and frost, thrive in this area. In the best years, the wheat produced 24 times more seed than was originally sown, 30 times more white rye, 60 times more barley, and an incredible 300 times more millet, something difficult to believe for those who had never witnessed it. Concerning oats, Moldavia was not such a great producer as it was with other grains, nor was it a major consumer, as horses were typically fed with barley. In Lower Moldavia, millet grew incredibly well, leading to a proverb that said that the millet of Lower Moldavia and the apples of Upper Moldavia don't have skins. After they crushed, ground, and baked it like a loaf of bread, many locals used to eat it with butter while still warm. Here you won't find orchards, but forests of fruit trees. In the mountains, the fruits grew without human intervention, but in the fields, they had to be cultivated and cared for by farmers, which is why the fruits were even tastier. Besides, their yield was so abundant that in the past, when the Poles planned to invade Moldavia, they considered there was no need for provisions, as these regions would provide them with all of the necessary food. However, after repeatedly suffering from various illnesses due to their excessive consumption of fruits and experiencing a huge loss without even engaging with their enemies, they realized it would be wiser to buy the necessary food instead. The other bounties of the earth were surpassed by the wonderful grapevines, which stretch from Cotnari to the Danube, being so fruitful that only one acre, which spans up to 24 poles, produces around 400-500 measures of 40 pounds of wine each. The noblest wine is fabricated at Cotnari, a town of the land of Hîrlău. Foreigners were unaware of it, for without proper transportation by sea or land, the wine lost its potency, even if I would dare affirm that it was more refined and superior to any other European wine, including the Tokai. However, if kept in a deep stone cellar, as was the local custom, by the fourth year it gained such strength, that it burned like hot brandy. The most wine-tolerant person could only handle three glasses of this wine before becoming drunk, but without getting a hangover. The wine's color was peculiar, unlike any other wine, taking on a greenish hue. The older the wine, the more pronounced its green tint became.

Beyond this point, toward the northern parts of the country, there are no more vineyards that can produce fine wines, because, in this part of the Cotnari hills, none of the grapevines ever reached maturity despite repeated attempts to do so. Nature, by depriving the vineyards in the neighboring northern areas of their wine-producing potential, seems to have concentrated its power in only one spot. The second-best wine in Moldavia is made in Huși, in the land of Falcău; the third place belonged to the one from Odobești, in the region of Putna on the Milcov River; the fourth-best wine was from Nicorești in the region of Tecuci, on the Siret River; the fifth place was reserved for the wine from Greci, in the region of Tutova, on the Berheci River and, finally, the sixth place is awarded to the wine produced in the fields of Costești, in the exact same land mentioned above. These vineyards not only catered to the locals, but drew even the attention of foreign merchants, including Russians, Poles, Czechs, Transylvanians, and even Hungarians. Their affordable prices made the vineyards a popular destination, with large quantities of wine being exported every year to their respective countries, even though the quality of the produce was not always the highest. Long ago, during the Moldavian rule of Bessarabia, the region had impressive vineyards. However, after the arrival of the Turks who did not drink wine, led to a decline in the wine culture. Nevertheless, the Christians who live in Chilia and Ismail continue to take care of vineyards, even if they barely produce enough for their daily consumption.

Moldavia has beautiful forests, with some containing firewood, and others fruit-bearing trees. Sailors have a special fondness for Moldavian oak tree wood, considering it superior and more resistant to rot than any other type of wood for ship construction. However, they also knew that the white bark inside the tree has to be carefully removed, as failure to do so would cause the wood to rot quickly. If it is adequately removed, this type of wood can resist for up to 100 years, undamaged by storms, air, or water. Two of these oak tree forests are better known than the rest: Cotnari and Tigheciu. The Cotnari Forest, near the town of that same name, is man-made. During the reign of Stephen the Great, there was a large field on this spot, that stretched over the entire area. When the Poles with their army made camp there, Stephen the Great attacked and defeated them, sent them running with all of their things, cutting down many of them and taking more than twenty thousand captives, most of them nobles. In exchange for them, the Polish king offered a significant sum of money as ransom, but Stephen refused it. He did not desire money; instead, he wanted a triumphant achievement to immortalize and proclaim his victories for future generations. With this goal in mind, he forced the Poles into hard physical labor, compelling them to till the entire battlefield that spanned two miles in length and one mile in width. He then cultivated it with acorns which created this beautiful forest. The Moldavians today call it "Dumbrăvile Roşii," as it had been watered with Polish blood. The Poles call it Bucovina and they always grieve when they remember it.

The other forest, located beyond the Prut River at the border with Bessarabia, is called Tigheci and has a circumference of almost 30 Italian miles. It was the strongest bastion of Moldavia against the Scythians, who tried to conquer it but never succeeded. The trees, though they are tall, are so dense that no man can walk through them without following a well-known path, familiar only to the locals. Once, this area had up to twelve thousand residents, the bravest soldiers of Moldavia. However, after numerous battles and massacres on both sides, the population had dwindled to a mere two thousand. They had a treaty with the Tartars from Buceag, their neighbors. They agreed to give them a number of tree trunks every year because Bessarabia did not have many forests. This agreement is still in place today;

Occasionally, the Tartars would violate the terms of their agreement and demand more than what was previously agreed upon. In such cases, the locals would take up arms to resist them, often emerging victorious. I will delve further into this matter later.

Chapter VII
About the Wildlife and Domestic Animals of Moldavia

I have no intention to engage in a lengthy description of the animals of Moldavia and the neighboring areas. My purpose is not to recall the stags, deer, goat herds, or the foxes, lynxes, and wolf packs. I only want to portray what I observed to be unique about Moldavian animals.

First of all, I remember that locally there are three types of sheep: those from the mountains, those from Soroca, and the wild ones. One could hardly tell how numerous and how large the herds that could be seen roaming all over the mountains were. Given that the western part of Moldavia was not ideal for the cultivation of cereals, sheep raising was the primary occupation of the residents and a vital source of sustenance. From this place, every year, 60,000 sheep just like the ones mentioned, were taken to Constantinople by Greek merchants (the Turks called them Kyvirgic) for the Sultan's kitchens. Their meat was favored by the Turks because of its taste and its ease of preparation. They had found the best grasslands in three places: Russian Câmpulung, on the water stream of Putila, Moldavian Câmpulung, on the Moldavia River, and in the land of Putna, in the Vrancea Mountains. In the lowlands, you could find much larger sheep than those from the mountains, but not as many; among the ones that deserve to be mentioned was the variety that reproduced their species in the land of Soroca. All of them had one extra rib, which they never lost; but if they were taken to another region, in their third year they gave birth to a lamb with the normal number of ribs. Similarly, if a sheep from another region was brought into this area, by the third year, the lamb born to that sheep would have an additional rib compared to its mother. Of all the sheep species, the wild sheep in this region are undoubtedly the most extraordinary, and I believe they cannot be found anywhere else. Their lower lip droops down for about two palms, which means that they have to graze by backing up a bit. Their necks are exceptionally short and lack joints, so they cannot turn their heads left or right. Despite their short legs, they are remarkably fast and can outrun dogs. Also, they have an excellent sense of smell, allowing them to detect hunters or other animals up to a German mile away, but only if the wind is blowing in their direction. If the wind is blowing from the opposite direction, they cannot detect anything, and that's when they are most vulnerable to being caught.

Just like this, the people who live in mountainous regions have small bulls, and the residents of the lowlands own big and beautiful oxen, from which more than 40,000 were taken through Poland, to Danzig, and from there, sold in the neighboring areas with the name of Polish-native bulls. In Moldavia, a pair of these animals costs 5 imperials, and in the winter the price drops to 3 imperials, while in Gedanum (Danzig), I discovered their price is 40-50 imperials. The fattest and most impressive bulls are raised near the tiny Sărata River, in the land of Fălciu, and around the Başeu stream, in the land of Cernăuți, because these fields have high salt levels and tender grass, which helps them stay fat. Their importance is so great that the residents can sustain their lives only by taking care of these animals, but it also allows them to pay the high taxes demanded by the Turks.

Around both shores of the Dniester River wild buffalo can be frequently seen; these animals don't seem to be native to the region, but to Podolia and the Tartar country, as they were forced to cross the Dniester River, frozen by the northern winds that blow across those regions in the winter.

In the western mountains, lives another animal that, I almost dare to say, only exists in our region. The Moldavians call it an "auroch." It is the size of a domestic bull, but its head is smaller and more elongated, its neck slimmer, and its stomach flatter, its legs are longer, horns are thinner and straighter, very sharp and bent slightly outward. It is a wild and fast animal and, just like the goats, it can climb mountain slopes, which is why this animal is hard to kill or harm without a gun. This is the same animal whose head Dragoș, the first ruler of Moldavia after its founding, choose to make the emblem of the country.

In the land of Orhei, in the village of Tohatin, between the Ichel and Răut Rivers, the pigs are not born with their hoofs split, but with round ones, just like horses; the same thing happens to piglets born here after three years to sows brought here from other regions; this doesn't only apply to domesticated piglets, but also in the wild ones, that reproduce a lot in the reeds surrounding the Dniester River.

Moldavian horses from the mountain areas are smaller and they almost resemble Ruthenian ones, but they are very robust, capable of hard work, and have such hard hoofs that, even when walking on extremely difficult paths, there is no need to put horseshoes on them. However, the lowland regions have more remarkable horses, that are famous for their beauty, speed, and endurance, and appreciated, not only by the Poles and the Hungarians but also by the Turks, who have a saying: "*Acem dilberi Bogdan bargiri meșhurdar,*" which means "A young Persian and a Moldavian horse are more laudatory than anything else." Near the borders with Bessarabia large herds of wild horses can be seen, which do not differ in any way from the domestic ones except for the fact that they are a little smaller and their hoofs are wider than a palm, round, and very strong. As autumn approaches and the region is soaked by incessant rains, gradually turning into a swamp, the Scythians (Tartars) from Buceag choose a day and a place and fill all the surrounding fields with howls and screams. Upon hearing these cries, the horses begin to run in every direction through the noisy fields, trying to find a quiet place. Eventually, they gather in the middle of a muddy ground called a *göller*. In that spot, unable to run because their large hoofs are trapped in mud, the Tartars attack them with arrows and spears. Some of the horses are captured alive, while many are killed in the process. Afterward, all of them are divided up as the Tartars see fit.

I am going to omit other forms of wildlife. Our forests are full of lynxes, martens (not the ones that are usually called "sables") and foxes, etc., whose furs protect us against the frost. I will mention a few details about the bees because the things I noticed about them as an observer were not unpleasant or widely known by everyone.

The residents derive great benefits from the bees, as the fields and forests are filled with splendid flowers that provide the raw material for honey and wax. They could reap even greater rewards if they could maintain a higher number of bee colonies each year. However, the country's regulations forbid individuals from having more beehives than their land can support, so as not to disturb their neighbors. In addition to the usual honeycombs, the bees produce a specific type of wax with a strong odor and a blackish color. This wax is not used to store honey, but rather to keep sunlight away.

In this context, when beekeepers capture a new colony with their Queen bee and transfer it to a primitive hive, they drill specific holes and make cracks. Since bees can only work in the dark, they first seal these openings with the blackish wax mentioned earlier, before attending to other tasks. After this, they begin their regular activities. From time to time, the beekeepers remove this wax along with the honey, and because of its amber smell and resistance to sunlight, they sell it at a higher price. Observations have shown that when swarms of bees are close to each other, or when they meet in the air, they engage in fierce fighting until one of the sides retreats, and is considered the loser. The winning swarm doesn't choose the pollen from the flowers and fields anymore, but enters the hives of the defeated colony and takes the honey, something that the losing side cannot refuse. If a beekeeper notices that his bees have been working hard but without any gain, he mixes chalk with water and sprays it on all his hives. The next day, he visits the neighboring beekeeper whose bees were suspected of causing the damage and shows him the white spots. This forces the neighbor to repair the damage.

In Moldavia and at the border of Pocuția, there is a bird called *ieruncă* by the locals or *glușca* by the Poles. Both of the names mean "deaf." It resembles a wild hen, but it is smaller, dumber, and deaf. If a hunter comes across a tree with a hundred of these birds, he could shoot them one by one, as the remaining ones watch their kin fall. The meat of these birds is very white and tender, superior to that of a partridge or a pheasant.

Part II
Politics

Chapter I
About the Organization of the Moldavian State

Those who wish to describe the political structure of the Moldavian state, should, in my view, first investigate how this state is governed, because I have seen even the most learned scholars describe it incorrectly. The clearest evidence concerning it, recorded by reliable ancient historians, was that previously the whole of Dacia, after it was transformed into a Roman province, was governed by Roman magistrates, according to Roman laws. After the decline of the Empire, because the Romans no longer sent troops or rulers to the province, and because of a lack of soldiers and local leaders, the Italian inhabitants could not hold out against the endless Barbarian attacks, they took examples from the neighboring nations that I previously mentioned, apparently giving all power to one man. The dense fog that obscures all the historical events of those centuries prevents us from explaining in more detail the way things occurred. What is certain is that the inhabitants of Moldavia, who had Roman origins, and had sought refuge in the mountains because of attacks by the Scythians and other barbarians, always maintained kings or rulers of their own. From this line descended that well-known John, mentioned by Nicetas Choniates, as leader of the Wallachians, from which Bogdan, the son of Dragoş, the first who had led our nation to return to their original land, had received the same rank from those who followed him to Moldavia. His descendants maintained their leadership, some through inheritance, others through election by the leaders of the country, with so much authority that even though they could not compare themselves to other Christian princes in matters of strength and the expanse of the conquered nations, they were not below them in terms of power and rights concerning their people. They did not lack any of the prerogatives of supreme power, elements used by princes to boast about themselves. Except for God and their sword, they did not acknowledge anyone more powerful in their country; they were not linked to any foreign prince as vassals or by a vow of faith; war, peace, life, death, and every resident's goods depended on their will and the leader could decide anything concerning them as he saw fit, right or wrong, without anyone resisting. Finally, John Paleologus, the Emperor of Constantinople, granted Alexander the Good the royal diadem and the title of despot, in the time of the Council of Florence (Leunclavius, *Pandect*, Chapter 71).[29] Whenever an enemy attacked, the whole nation, at the command of the ruler, was bound to take up arms and avenge the foes. This was how Moldavia stood up and defended itself not only from attacks by the Poles and Transylvanians but also against the wrath of the Turks; moreover, under the leadership of Stephen the Great[30], after all the enemies, from all

---

[29] Cantemir is incorrect about the timing of this. Alexander the Good died in 1432 and the Council of Florence took place in 1439.

[30] *Author's Note:* It was quoted about this ruler from Dlugosz's testimonials, the Polish historian: "Oh, wonderful man," said him "with nothing below the heroic army commandants which we admired so much, which close to our times had won the first world's principle, a so bright victory over the Turks, the most worthy by my judgment, which should be entrusted with the leadership of the whole country and, especially, to become the supreme commandant of the army against the Turks. In my opinion and also in the consent and decision of every Christian resident, as other princes and Catholic kings exhausted themselves with misunderstandings, cravings, or wars, this may be the best option (Lib.13, page 513, year 1474). On page 532, he called Stephen: "the most awaken, brightest and the most significant

directions, were beaten back, Moldavia had expanded its boundaries into enemy territories. His reign represented the most fortunate era for Moldavia and its peak, after which it started slowly to decline until it reached its actual condition of poverty. Under the rule of his son, Bogdan, the strength of Moldavia, the prince's absolute power and right to declare war or to make peace had quickly disappeared; all this happened after the former ruler took an oath of loyalty to the Turks and promised to pay the Sultan four thousand *guldens* annually, as a sign of vassalage. Some shadow of it remained for a time and it seemed that the nation stood under the protection of the Turks instead of being controlled by them; this might have happened because this state didn't want to incite the already rebellious souls of their new subjects and because they were afraid that the people they wanted to become their serfs could turn into rebellious enemies. The ancient lineage of Drăgoșești came to an end with the death of Stephen, the son of Peter Rareș, the ambitions of the nobles who disputed who would assume the throne offered the Turks a great opportunity: they started to impose ever larger tributes and despoil them of the freedom they had maintained until then. As time went on, the Turks also abolished the right of the boyars to choose their own ruler,

---

Prince and Warrior." There were more of these kinds of praising words from this author. Stanislas Orichovius, a Polish historian as well, said: "These people, by their nature, traditions, and language did not differ much from the Italian lifestyle: they were fierce (in battle) and braver than any other nation, taking into account the glory of war and the courage; these two elements assured their resistance, even if their country was tiny, to the attacks of the neighboring enemy countries, which attacked or fought them. Their valor was so grand that they managed to fight against all the neighboring nations at once and pulled everything through. Indeed Stephen, who had the leadership of Dacia in the period of our parents, had defeated Bayezid the Turk, Matthias the Hungarian, and John Albert the Pole, almost in a single summer." (Annal. 5., year 1552)

and they brought whatever foreign princes they wanted to rule. By replacing those in positions of power and then reinstating them, they created confusion. These tactics were employed to such an extent that the Ottoman Porte came to hold almost all of the rights of supreme power that had previously belonged to local rulers. I cannot deny that the most significant cause of this misfortune was the ambition of several outlandish rulers who had no hesitation to promise or give to the Turks anything, instead of appreciating their statute; when the ordinary tributes were no longer sufficient, they had to figure out new ways to pay. That is how Moldavia, a country that had only experienced one type of political misfortune, which was manageable, ended up with doubled problems, and suffering due to the Turks and foreign rulers. To include everything in a few words, in this kind of trouble, the wise Turkish Emperors had assimilated whatever they considered profitable for themselves; on the contrary, anything that they did not hope to be useful for them, they gave away to the rulers, to caress at least some of the ambitious candidates' souls. The rights of proclaiming war, declaring peace, making agreements, and sending emissaries to neighboring princes regarding state business were taken away from the Moldavian rulers, even though they were left with their absolute freedom and almost the same former power to establish laws, punish the residents, choose the boyars, impose taxes, and they could even elect the bishop and fill other positions like this. The sovereignty of the ruler extended not only to Moldavian officials and citizens but also to Turkish merchants and people of all social classes residing in the territory. Their life or death remained in his hands. If he declared someone guilty to be punished with execution, beaten with rods, exiled, or confiscation of their assets, even if all of that would be done tyrannically and unfairly, the ones that were the subjects of these treatments could send him petitions for forgiveness, but no one could say anything against them or oppose the realization of the ruler's desire; contrariwise, if he wanted to spare someone from the death sentence proclaimed by the whole nation, nobody could oppose his will or drag the subject to the rack, so long as the victim was protected by him. All of the civil and military governors depended on his will: the ones dear to him received more, and those who he couldn't stand were charged. In this grant, there were no rules to follow for the ruler. If he had desired to give an ordinary peasant the highest rank that the Moldavian country could offer, the role of chancellor, no one would have dared to publicly share a different opinion; if he had wanted to flay someone who came from a very significant family from this rank, that person would have been subjected to the will of his ruler. He had the same power over not only the lower-ranking clerics, but also over the metropolitans, bishops, archimandrites, abbots, and anyone in the religious sphere if they had committed any injustice, anything that could harm the nation, whatever plan against the ruler or the state; without the accord of the Parliament of Constantinople he could easily take their job and ecclesiastical rank, not also the priestly one, and even sentence them to death. While it was true that the clerics selected their leader, they could only do so when summoned by the ruler and after obtaining his approval. The ruler would personally bestow the pastoral staff upon the chosen one, symbolizing that they did not belong to any other Christian prince except the Russian Emperor, having been removed from the jurisdiction of the Roman Emperor's Pope. These were the rights of the ruler over the Moldavian inhabitants, recognized not only by the Ottoman Court but also strengthened by various Emperors with several diplomas. Conversely, the leader had no such great power over the residents' goods. Forsooth, howsoever heavy taxes did he think of putting over the country, no one could oppose or not comply without the risk of losing his head; he was being forced to declare everything he collected to the Ottoman Court. Such was life in those times, when even if there was no trial against a person who had spilled innocent blood and the Grand Vizier was aware of it, he still faced great danger, especially when the entire country was burdened by the power of the boyars. If he had been proven to be guilty, the exile and confiscation of his fortune was usually the punishment, because only rebellion or denial of paying the annual tribute could attract the death sentence. This hindrance had not been so powerful to be prevented from being violated. Actually, if the ruler had properly tamed the Vizier with gifts, Pasha, Defterdar, and the others that enjoyed living in the same society as the leader, had no reason to be scared of the complaints of the boyars or the whole nation, as no problem could be not sustained at the Turkish court by a defender, which knew how to attract justice to his side, with both hands full. This way, no matter how hard the tyranny of the Turks pushed Moldavia, the ruler could do whatever he wanted, without fear: no individual would defy his will unpunished. Overturning the decisions of the previous ruler or revisiting matters already judged by him was a daunting task, not only due to the laws but also because of the customs and traditions deeply ingrained in the nation. That was why, even if some leaders brought back on the account of the treasury lands that had been alienated by their predecessors, mostly justified as gifts those less dignified; this thing had never been approved by the state or didn't last for a long time, as the harmed ones always won from the successor of an unfair ruler and gained the return of their goods.

Chapter II
About the Election of the Rulers of Moldavia

After discussing the power of the Moldavian rulers, the order of things required us to do a more elaborate description of the actual and past election protocols. The indifference of our ancestors, to whom what mattered more was to do brilliant things instead of writing them down, had prevented us from establishing, step by step, right from our nation's formation, how these things took place; if only I was allowed to make presumptions, I would support, not without strong reasons, that the ancient leadership of Moldavia was hereditary and that the elections were useless until all aristocrats were dead. In addition to this perspective, there was a significant argument that contradicted the prevailing tradition among the formerly stronger European nations: even the first line of Moldavian leaders demonstrated that it was extremely difficult to relinquish power once an aristocratic dynasty had taken hold. To underscore this point, it is worthwhile to present a complete list of the Moldavian rulers, who had been in power until the present time.

Therefore, the first one who, after the invasion of Batie (Batuhan), brought back the former glory of Moldavia was Dragoş. Even though our analysis didn't reveal his genealogy, the tradition always said that he came from the lineage of the ancient Moldavian rulers, having Bogdan as his father, the son of John. This custom seemed to be worthier to be believed, as it would be hard to imagine that an ordinary person could have brought a group so numerous to the hunt that enabled him to discover Moldavia, and to convince the people to follow him; after Dragoș, these other rulers followed:

2. Sas;

3. Lațco, the son of Sas;

4. Bogdan I, called Mușat. Because he died without an heir, he was followed by his paternal uncle;

5. Peter I, the uncle of Bogdan Mușat, who also died without having any children and was followed by his paternal uncle;

6. Roman I, the son of Lațcu who was the brother of Mușat. After his death, because Alexander, his son, was not at an age of leadership or because of a rebellion, the chosen one was

7. Stephen I, followed by his son

8. Peter the Second (II), who was followed by

9. Stephen the Second (II), brother of Peter and son of Stephen I, who was brutally banished from the leadership by

10. Iuga. However, his dominion was not long, and before he reached one year of rule, he was unfairly unseated by

11. Alexander I, also called "the Good," son of Roman I. Through him, the old bloodline of Drăgoșești was reinstated in its rights. He was the one who made the name of the Moldavian nation known for the first time, as until then the country's name was not well-known. He sent the Moldavian Metropolitan to the Council of Florence, along with other delegates, and by strongly defending the orthodoxy, John Palaiologos, the Emperor of Constantinople, gifted him not

only the title of Despot, but also a royal crown.[31] He was followed by his son

12. Ilie I, who was followed by his brother

13. Stephen the Third (III), the son of Alexander I. He was the first to usurp the right of the ruler's son and claimed leadership only after his brother's death. I have observed that this has happened several times throughout Moldavia's history. The reason for this incident was that Alexander I, having been removed from his position of ruler due to Stefan I's election, could not regain his former status without the support of the boyars. That was the time when Moldavian boyars had more freedom in choosing their ruler, yet were restricted by the condition of choosing their new ruler from the noble bloodline, unless there was already an existent one, as things had formerly been done in the election of Polish Kings and the ways that were currently applied in the choosing of Turkish Sultans and the Hans from Crimea. After all this, the crown went to

14. Roman the Second (II), son of Ilie I, but along with his death, the crown went to

15. Peter the Third (III), who was followed by his son

16. Stephen the Fourth (IV), who was followed by

17. Alexander the Second (II), son of Ilie I and brother of Roman the Second (II); after his death, the crown went to his son,

18. Bogdan II, who was followed by his brother

19. Peter the Fourth (IV), called Aron, the son of Alexander the Second. After he died, the crown went to

---

[31] See note 29.

20. Stephen the Fifth (V), named "the Great," the son of Bogdan the Second (II), a ruler beyond any praise and the most vigorous defender of his country against all enemy attacks, from whatever side; after him, the crown went to

21. Bogdan the Third (III), who because of an eye defect was called "the Blind" or "the Dim," the person who gave Moldavia to the Turks. By allowing this to happen, he became the first to cause the misfortune currently afflicting Moldavia. He left the rulership of the country to his son at the moment of his death.

22. Stephen the Sixth (VI), also called "the Young." He died without having any descendants and was followed by

23. Peter the Fifth (V), usually called Rareș or Majă, son of Stephen the Fifth (V), born from an illegitimate relationship. The election clearly demonstrated the extent to which the former boyars adhered to the succession of their ruler's descendants. No one knew the reason for Peter's birth, whether it was due to his parents' shame over guilty intercourse, or because the ruler did not wish to create conditions for future divisions after his death. Peter himself, unwitting of his noble origins, lived in such poor conditions that he was forced to live day by day with an ordinary job: fish trade (in the usual Moldavian vocabulary, it was called "măjărie," which was the origin of his nickname of Majă). After Stephen the Sixth died, everyone knew that the lineage of Drăgoșești had gone extinct, and the boyars gathered to choose a new leader. That was the exact moment when the mother of Peter showed up and presented a will (or *uric*) of Stephen the Great, in which he stated she was to be exempted from taxes and recognized her son as his child; they were so excited by the news that, without any other deliberation, they chose Peter as ruler, as the descendent of their former ruler and summoned him from the fish trade to the throne. After several years he was removed by Suleiman

I, the Turkish Emperor, with the accusation of burning Chilia, and the throne was claimed by:

24. Stephen the Seventh (VII), who pretended to be the grandson of Alexander the Second (II), and, and used this claim to obtain support for his claim to rule over Moldavia from Suleiman and the boyars. His reign did not last long, as he was murdered by the boyars, who had plotted against him, and Peter Rareş again claimed the throne. After his death, the crown went to his son

25. Ilie the Second (II), who was followed by his brother, as he did not have any children.

26. Stephen the Eighth (VIII), also one of the sons of Peter the Fifth (V), died without heirs and put an end to the Drăgoşeşti lineage, clean or cross-bred. The extinction of this bloodline was the source and the main cause of several misfortunes that befell Moldavia. With no single noble bloodline to surpass others and to maintain order by keeping troublemakers in check, the country became divided and rife with factions. The Turks paid little heed to these internal conflicts, knowing that Moldavia would be easier to rule if weak and divided. Within months, the Moldavians had installed and deposed several leaders. Eventually, the wisest among them came to an agreement and chose a leader adorned with the signs of authority. This was

27. Peter the Steward (Stolnicul – a name coming from *stolnic*, meaning the one who was in charge of the royal feasts) of the deceased ruler Stephen. At his enthronement, he was given the name of Alexander the Third (III), also called Lăpuşneanu. Against him, from the opposite party, the next one was forced to take the throne

28. Despot, usually named by our historians "The Heretic," a cunning and polyglot man, with the help of the Turks, banished Alexander from the throne. Aware of the enmity that many harbored towards him, and having survived several previous assassination attempts, he decided to fake his own death. To this end, he arranged

for a man bearing a strong resemblance to himself to be buried in his place. He fled to Poland in secret, hoping to gain deeper insight into the plans of his fellow conspirators. After his departure, the Moldavians requested again for Alexander Lăpușneanu to rule, but his joy did not last for long. Returning from Poland, Despot didn't come alone, but with a strengthened army aided by the Poles who supported him. He banished Alexander again and forced him to leave the throne. Lastly, after his death, the crown was forcibly given to

29. Stephen the Ninth (IX) Tomșa, who was formerly a *hatman*, a commander of the army. It was not a long time until the Moldavians became disgusted by his wicked rule and asked again for Alexander for the third time, from Poland, where he had been hiding. He was a just ruler before, and he fought and defeated Stephen and took his head. After all of these trials of destiny, he had a better rule, and died on the throne, leaving his heir both riches and the throne

30. Bogdan the Fourth (IV), his son. Because this one died without having any descendants, the boyars chose

31. John the Armenian,[32] called this because of the tradition of the Armenians, in which they ate meat during the abstinence period of the Apostles. He was very knowledgeable of Greek and Latin languages, a former colleague of John Lascaris, whose letters sent to him can be currently seen in the *Turco-Graecia* book, written by Crusius. As he could not stand tyranny and desired freedom, he was strategically caught by the Turks and torn apart by camels. As a descendant of his, the Turks decided to give the crown to

32. Peter the Sixth (VI), also called "The Lame," son of Mircea, the leader of Muntenia. However, the Moldavian boyars could hardly tolerate the rule of a stranger, and not long after they started plotting,

---

[32] Also known as John the Brave or John the Terrible, Prince of Moldavia, 1572-1574.

About the Election of the Rulers of Moldavia

they removed him with the Turks' help. They then gave the throne to

33. Iancul, being part of the Saxon community, who, I don't know how convinced many people that he was a descendant of the Drăgoșești bloodline. As he incurred the hatred of the entire population due to his debauchery and inhumanity, he eventually ended up being killed by an alliance of boyars. In his place, for the second time, came

Peter the Sixth (VI), the Lame, who, seeing that he was hated, and preferred peace to glory, abdicated and retired to his private life, moving away to Transylvania. The abandoned throne was, by the choice of the boyars, given to

34. Aron, a cruel and savage man. After he was deposed by the Moldavians for his tyranny, and for giving Bender to the Turks, the Sultan helped him get reinstated. After his death came

35. Stephen the Tenth (X), called Răzvan, was the ruler of Moldavia for some time. After him, the throne went to

36. Ieremia Movilă, but after his death, it was inherited by his brother

37. Simion Movilă. After his death, Moldavia had three rulers from the same lineage at the same time

38. Michael the First (I), son of Simion Movilă;

39. Constantine the First (I);

40. Bogdan the Fifth (V), brother of Constantine the First, the sons of Ieremia Movilă; each one of them, because they planned to make important changes and surrender the country to the Poles, were banished by the boyars, who didn't want the support of the Poles. By this act of faith, they easily achieved from the Turks the right to replace the former rulers with one of their choosing.

41. Stephen the Eleventh (XI) Tomșeivici, received the throne. He was followed by

42. Gașpar, Italian by nationality, had formerly been a *dragoman* at the Ottoman court. He took the throne of Moldavia by force; because he tried to convert Moldavia to the Catholic religion, the boyars disposed of him, and the Turks found a replacement for him:

43. Radul, with the nickname of "Lungul" (the Tall), had formerly been the ruler of Wallachia; after his death, the throne was given by the boyars to:

44. Miron Barnovski, Polish by nationality, who was welcomed into the Moldavian nobility due to his long service. During his leadership, the election of the ruler, which had always been the right of the boyars, was completely taken over by the Turks by the ruler's decision, without anyone considering the opinion of the nobility. As the war started between the Polish and Ottoman Courts after Miron switched to the enemy's side, a thing that attracted a terrible attack on Moldavia by the Tartars, the boyars, to stop the potential suffering of the country, allowed the Turks to choose the ruler, with only two conditions: his religion had to be Orthodox and he had to be a noble. Because of this, after Barnovski was beheaded (as we will mention in more detail later), the Turks chose as the ruler of Moldavia:

45. Alexander the Fourth (IV), called the Iliaș, who was believed to be from the bloodline of Stephen the Fifth (V). After his death, they chose:

46. Moise, son of Simion Movilă, was honored, something out of the ordinary, with three horse tails. However, after his death, the Turks disregarded all agreements and laws and rarely appointed sons of former leaders or even native Moldavians to the position of ruler. Instead, they sometimes appointed foreigners. In this way, against the will of the country's boyars, by giving the Turks a lot of money, the throne was bought by:

47. Vasile, originally from Epirus, who wanted to keep his nickname as "Lupul" (the Wolf) even after his coronation. The locals patiently suffered under his rule for many years, but finally, they banished him, replacing him with:

48. Stephen the Twelveth (XII), also called "Burduja" (the Fat). His reign was supported by the Ottoman Court. Because he became an ally of the Polish, the throne passed on to:

49. Gheorghe Ghica, an Albanian, who was a *capuchehaia*, Stephen's official representative at the Ottoman Court. The Turks decided to assign him as the ruler of Moldavia. After he switched thrones to rule Wallachia, Moldavia was entrusted by the Turks to:

50. Stephen the Thirteenth (XIII), the son of Vasile the Albanian. After his death, the local boyars and the Turks gave the throne to:

51. Eustratie Dobija. After his death, with the Turks' help, the throne was taken by:

52. Ilie the Thrid (III), son of Alexander the Forth (IV), called "Ilias." After he was dethroned by the people who gave it to him, he was followed by:

53. Duca, the Greek. He was common-born, but thanks to his qualities not only did he manage to become one of the best Moldavian rulers, but also married the daughter of Eustratie Dobija. Anyway, he was dethroned by the Turks after only six months, and replaced by Ilie the Third (III); the latter was the only one who was dethroned once, but reinstated. However, not long after that, Duca became ruler once again. Because the Moldavians complained starting with the Camnița expedition, the next one to be chosen was:

54. Stephen the Fourteenth (XIV) Petriceicu. Because he switched to the Polish side right in the middle of the battle of Hotin, the Moldavian throne was bought from the Sultan with a silver fountain by:

55. Dumitrașcu Cantacuzino, who, after being exiled from Wallachia, traded expensive gemstones in Constantinople. After his removal, the reign was given to the *capuchehaia*.

56. Antonie Roset, a nobleman from Constantinople. After him, Duca the Greek was crowned for the third time by the Turks; after the Poles captured him, Dumitrașcu Cantacuzino was chosen for the second time, even if he was hated by the other boyars for his tyranny. Still, they made a treaty with the Ottoman Court and earned the right to choose their ruler again. This was the reason the next ruler got the crown.

57. Constantine the Second (II) Cantemir, also named the "the Elder." With his death, the crown passed to his younger son with the blessing of the boyars.

58. Dimitrie Cantemir was anointed by two patriarchs in the county of Iași; however, because he didn't receive the approval of the Ottoman Court, Cantemir was forced to give the crown to:

59. Constantine the Third (III), the son of Duca, who was forced by the Turks to rule; after he was removed with the help of a multitude of boyars' complaints, the Turks decided to give this duty to:

60. Antioh Cantemir, the older son of Constantine the Second (II), knew his brother's position was chosen by the Sultan himself, but his brother abdicated and let him have the throne. However, five years later, Constantine Brâncoveanu bought the throne from him with a huge sum of money, which was enough to quench the vizier's greed. The throne was taken by his son-in-law.

Constantine the Third (III), son of Duca, was, for the second time, the ruler of Moldavia. After a reign of two years and a half years, he was deposed by the boyars' reclamations. In order to replace him, the Turks decided to reinstate:

About the Election of the Rulers of Moldavia 83

Antioh Cantemir; Constantine Brâncoveanu, the greatest enemy of the Cantemir bloodline, bribed the Turks again with money to have him removed. The one who replaced him was:

61. Michael the Second (II) Racoviță, who married Elisaveta, the daughter of Constantine Cantemir. He was accused of treachery by Silistra's Turkish army commander (called a *seraschier*), so the Turks removed him from the throne, and replaced him with:

62. Nicolae Mavrocordat, once a *dragoman* of the Ottoman Court. He was the heir, in both blood and rank, of the famous Alexander Mavrocordat. However, as the peace between Russians and Turks started to fail and because he was thought to be a better writer than a fighter, he was removed from the throne and replaced with:

Dimitrie Cantemir, for the second time, who abandoned each honor and benefit and switched all of his armies to the Christians' side. His successor was:

Nicolae Mavrocordat, who was his predecessor as well. He was liked by the Turks and their priest because of his religion. For this, he was rewarded with the Wallachian throne, and the crown of Moldavia was given to Michael Racoviță. It was his second reign, and currently, he is trying to keep Moldavia as obedient as he can.

I became particularly invested in this chapter because I couldn't think of a more concise way to present all of these changes. To the kind reader, each of these developments was not straightforward to understand, as each one had left its mark on the circumstances and conditions of Moldavia. Indeed, if the reader would examine carefully the list of our country's rulers, which I composed earlier, he would observe on his own that:

1. Starting with Dragoș, the founder of Moldavia, and ending with Stephen the Great, as long as Moldavia was free, the right of succession was always respected;

2. This tradition remained unchanged even after the disappearance of the Dragoşeşti bloodline when the Turks ruled us;

3. After the bloodline disappeared, until the rise of the Movileşti family, the Moldavian boyars were free to choose their rulers;

4. The Moldavians always gave the throne to someone who was a relative of a former ruler;

5. After the rebellion of John the Armenian and Aron's betrayal, the Turks first took control of choosing the ruler, and eventually even the nomination process. As a result, anyone who was not the son of a ruler had a difficult time ascending to power and ruling the country.; and finally,

6. After the riot of Miron Barnovski, not only did that rule become outdated, but also the rank of the leader was auctioned by the Ottoman Court to ordinary outlanders.

I intended to provide a more detailed description of each of these events when the time came for a historical account of our country's destiny, covering everything from its founding to the present day.

Chapter III

Ancient and Present Customs Regarding the Enthronement of the Princes of Moldavia

After I showed you who was considered worthy back then and today to take over the throne of Moldavia, I consider it best to tell you something about the customs and the ceremonies practiced in ancient times when enthroning the princes. Following the enthronement of the first six princes, before choosing Stephen I and spoiling the hereditary succession that was respected up to then, few ceremonies were held, or none at all. Because the heir was known from the time when his father or brother were still alive, after the ruler's death, he needed only a proclamation to assume the throne. But as time passed and they started asking for a legal confirmation given by the vote of the boyars, many more solemnities had to be introduced. After the death of Roman I, the sixth ruler from the founding of Moldavia, his son, Alexander the Good, being of a very young age, wasn't capable of assuming the burden of ruling the country, and at the same time repelling enemies that were invading from every direction. As a result, the boyars decided to choose a knowledgeable ruler, skilled in the art of war instead of placing a child at the helm of the country and risking putting it in danger because of his ignorance.

At that time, that right belonged to every boyar, but because of the commotions arising more and more often caused by large numbers of voters, the right was later granted to the seven great boyars of the first rank which were: the *Great Logofăt*,[33] the two *vornici*,[34] the *hatman*,[35] the *postelnic*,[36] the *Great Spătar*,[37] and the *Great Paharnic*.[38]

Immediately following the death of the prince, they met in the *divan*[39] so that the country would not be without a ruler for too long. After reading the late prince's testament, if no successor was mentioned, they chose a new ruler through a majority of votes, which they would not make public. But if through a fatherly testament, one of the late ruler's sons was named as heir, the voters could not ignore the decision and no voting process followed.

With this done, they proceeded with the funeral and if, during his lifetime, he had built a monastery, they buried his remains in its

---

[33] The *logofăt* was the head of the prince's chancellery, responsible for drawing up correspondence and documents.

[34] The *vornic* served as a magistrate, having juridical functions which he exercised throughout the country.

[35] The *hatman* was the Prince's chief military officer.

[36] The *postelnic* was responsible for maintaining the Prince's household.

[37] The *spătar* a military officer, commander of the cavalry.

[38] The *păharnic* was responsible for the prince's wine cellars and for provisioning the court.

[39] The *divan* was the name of the royal council.

church. If not, they buried him in some other great church. After the funeral ended, every great boyar and nobleman, together with the heads of the army, returned from the church to the court in deep silence, wearing only dark clothing and with their expressions full of sorrow. Immediately following that, the great boyars entered the Grand Divan, and they took the same seats they had held during their late prince's life, while as many military units as possible stood in line in front of the divan, with their flags and arms pointing to the ground, waiting for the proclamation of the new prince. Meanwhile, if the named prince was the son of the late ruler, he would stand next to his father's throne, wearing mourning attire. However, if he was chosen by the great boyars, he would sit unmoving in his own seat that he had held before. After all of this being ordained, the first one to break the silence was the Metropolitan, and through a well-chosen speech, he recounted the merits of the deceased, lamenting his fate in the name of the whole country. After the speech, the *Great Logofăt* read aloud to the crowd the testament of the late ruler, so that if the named heir was a younger brother, passing over the older one, which happened a few times in the past, it would be known to all that this was the wish of the deceased and not the preference of the voters. Following the reading of the testament, the same logofăt was the first to approach the appointed prince and, if he was of noble birth, he would first try to soothe the pain caused by the death of his father or brother. He then announced that he was chosen through the testament of the deceased and he asked him in the name of all the provinces of Moldavia to take the Moldavian scepter as soon as possible and rule his subjects and ministers with a just and humane leadership.

At this, the new prince stood up, with his head bare, and usually answered using very few words, blaming fate for depriving the country of such a good ruler, mentioned that even if he was not worthy of carrying the burden of leadership, he could not disobey his father's or brother's command and the will of the whole country, and that was why he accepted the proffered honor, and that he would lead his subjects with righteousness, devotion, and gentleness. Following this, the crowd quickly stood up and the great retinue followed the new ruler to the Metropolitan Church, with the Metropolitan and the priests leading the way. At the door of the holy sanctuary, he was greeted with two candles by the Metropolitan swinging a censer at the entrance, and he was asked to kiss the cross and the Holy Bible, and was welcomed into the church after worship. After that, the ruler had to kneel at the altar in front of what they call the royal doors and lay his forehead on the *pristol* (holy table), where the Metropolitan, after putting the omophorion on his head, read aloud the prayers usually read at the coronations of Orthodox emperors and anointed him with holy oil. After these preliminary ceremonies were fulfilled, the ruler stood up and kissed the holy table at the altar and, successively, all the holy icons. At his return from the altar, in the middle of the church, the Metropolitan set a golden crown on his head, shining with precious stones, and while the cantors sang "He is worthy" (*vrednic este*), supporting him under his arms, the Metropolitan on the right side and the *Great Postelnic* on the left, they lifted him on a throne with three steps, towards the wall from the right side of the church. At the same time, the cannons around the city were fired and musicians, with the harmonious sounds of their instruments, proclaimed the day's celebration.

After he was ἀπολύσει, the ruler was then dressed at the church's entrance in a royal caftan, while the boyars removed the dark clothing they wore until then and replaced them with others, more cheerful and bright. All this being done, the ruler mounted his horse again and, followed by the Metropolitan, together with the whole council, returned to court, where, entering the grand hall, he climbed on the throne by himself, a solemnity during which the hem of his robe was held, as a custom, by the hatman or the head of the army on the right side and by the *Great Postelnic* on the left. Behind the ruler came the Metropolitan, together with the council. After they took their seats, the Metropolitan approached the ruler and, after kissing his hands, he held a short speech to wish him happiness and abundance in everything, telling him he would pray for him and, at the same time, asking him for protection for him and his clergy. Turning toward the people afterward, he blessed them all and asked them to have faith in their ruler. The Metropolitan was followed by the bishops of Moldavia and the clergy. After they all kneeled for their new ruler, they were received to kiss his hands and his royal caftan, and the *Great Logofăt*, together with the other boyars, each according to their rank, did the same. At the end of this ceremony, the ruler stood up from his throne, and, uncovering his head, he thanked everyone for the love they showed him, promising he would be a kind and just defender of the country. After the speech, the spătar placed the crown back on the ruler's head and retreated to what was called the secret room, while everyone else returned to their chores. The boyars' wives gave the same honors to the ruler's wife, if he was married, all of this in the lady's receiving chamber, separate from the coronation ceremony, which was a religious solemnity, unfit for a woman. Either way, she had a raised throne closer to the door of the church, which was shorter than her husband's, and in her receiving chambers (where all the wives, even those of the great boyars, each had their seat mirroring the rank of their husband) she wore a crown identical to her husband's, a fact that can be seen in old portraits.

This is the way the enthronement of Moldavia's ruler was done, but later everything was broken by the tyranny of the Turks and the right of the boyars to choose their ruler was taken away from them. The method of choosing the prince is now completely different. As soon as the vizier learns of the passing of Moldavia's ruler or he decides, out of hate or because of a fault of his, to remove him from the throne, he looks for a new ruler among the nobles' sons and other boyars from Constantinople, and if times are peaceful, he promises the throne to the one that offers the most money, but if there is a threat of war, to the one that is most loyal and well-known for his military merits. After he agrees with this candidate upon the gifts and other conditions of his new leadership, and after he receives in writing the sum of money he must pay, he lets the Emperor know of his intention through a letter called *talhîș*, written with similar wording: "The current ruler of Moldavia puts such oppression beyond measure on Your Majesty's subjects, that the boyars of that country were forced to flee to neighboring countries, to escape his oppression, some even came here begging for your royal mercy against such a cruel lord." (In cases where the ruler is to be removed, whether justly or unjustly, and he cannot be justly blamed, accusations are fabricated against him, such as failing to pay tribute or being negligent in fulfilling commands.) "Because this fact is completely against your majesty's and the empire's interests, I considered you should (if your majesty thinks the same) remove the above-named ruler from his throne and put another named person in his place, a person I know to be just, faithful, honest, and deserving of this favor." If this proposal pleases the Emperor and if neither the *cîzlar-agasî* nor other subjects of his intimate court oppose the vizier's attempts, he usually writes underneath in his own handwriting: *mucibince amel oluna* which means "to be done as you wrote above." After receiving this permission, the vizier, if he wants to work in secret, and if he is afraid that the ruler, finding out of his misfortune, might flee to Christian countries, calls the leading candidate to the court during the night, and if he doesn't have such fears, during the day, where he is welcomed with honor by the *chehaia-beg* of the Grand Vizier, and taken to the private chambers he owns at the vizier's court, where he is invited to sit. The *chehaia*, after saluting each other, shows him the reason he was summoned (even though the candidate knows very well, but the court's ceremony requires him to be informed again) and tells him that his master, the vizier, told the Sultan about the religious services of his father or his own and the services done for the Ottoman Empire and that through this he earned the honor of naming him Prince of Moldavia, advises him to appear worthy of this high rank, to prove himself a true man by serving with faith, and to be careful not to embarrass the vizier in front of the Emperor, through carelessness or lack of faith. Telling him all this, the *chehaia*, leaves the chambers and goes to the vizier's private room and announces that the pretender to the throne of Moldavia that was summoned is there and awaits the orders of his highness; as soon as he finishes other chores, the vizier orders the *capugilar-chehaiasî*, the great doorkeeper, to receive the new lord. Before entering the *arzodasî* or the audience chamber, the Prince waits in the antechamber for a short while, until the vizier's subjects and keepers take their seats on both sides of the chamber, depending on their ranks; after that, he is invited to enter, and after kissing the vizier's hand, who sits between pillows, as are the Turkish customs, on his right, standing, the *chehaia*, backing up a bit, remains standing straight up. Then the vizier, looking up and taking a grave expression, first greets him solemnly using the words *Hos geldin beg,* which means "welcome prince" and then says: "Our brilliant, most just, and most kind Emperor, seeing that the lord who ruled Moldavia until now is negligent in executing commands and is oppressing his subjects, has decided to remove him from his rank. Because I know you're a good man and honest and faithful to Ottoman authority, I asked him to allow you to take his place. And our most kind Emperor agreed to my requests and, taking pity on you, has given you the dominion of Moldavia. It will be your duty through your faith to acknowledge this great favor from our Emperor to you and to have the same friends as we do, the same enemies as we do, to rule your subjects with kindness, to defend the just, to have no mercy for those that commit injustice, to be satisfied with the earnings that the laws and customs of the country afford the ruler and not to extort anything more than that from your people, and the tribute owed to the Emperor and the *peșcheș* to be sent to the court at the appointed time. If you follow these things, you will forever enjoy (for the rest of your life) the Emperor's kindness, but if you will do things another way, you should know that your end cannot be any less miserable." The ruler, if he speaks Turkish well, replies to the vizier's words, and if he doesn't know it, through the grand *dragoman* of the court, thanks him for the undeserved kindness from the Emperor, and promises to respect everything he was ordered to do, vows to gladly sacrifice all his power, even his life, to serve his majesty and asks for the kindness of his imperial majesty to never depart from him. After speaking all of this, at the order of the vizier, the *capugilar-chehaiasî* brings the garment called a *caftan* and gives it first to the ruler to kiss it, then dresses him with it over the rest of his clothing. Dressed so, he approaches the vizier again, kisses his hand and the hem of his robe, and presents his *capuchehaia*, which is his permanent envoy to the court that accompanies him, and asks him to kindly take him under his protection. If the vizier agrees, he usually replies *ne hoş*, which means "very well," after which the *capuchehaia* is dressed in a caftan of the second rank.

After fulfilling these ceremonies, the lord kisses the vizier's hand for the third time, leaves the receiving chamber, and goes to *chehaia's* chamber. After a short time, the *chehaia* joins him, congratulates the ruler on his new reign, offers him coffee and sherbet (which is made from sugar melted in water), and discusses the reign and other random topics. While the ruler spends his time in there, the vizier's *imbrohor*, who presides over the stables, readies a beautifully decorated horse, and the head of the *ceauşi* with 24 of them and four of the vizier's pedestrian *şatîri*, together with other *agalari* of the vizier (high-ranking subjects) and *ici-agalarî*, which are the house servants, wait for the ruler to come out. As soon as the *chehaia* learns that everything is readied in the usual way, he commands that spices are brought for burning, to perfume the ruler with their smoke, which for Turks is a sign that someone is leaving, and they're saying goodbye. After kissing the *chehaia's* hand, he mounts his horse, with a retinue of four *ceauşi* ahead of him, and they leave the vizier's court in the following order: the first to go are the *ceauşi*, as many as the ruler wishes, together with *ceauşlar-emini*, or their commander, followed by the vizier's *agalari* and *ici-agalarî*, behind them comes the ruler surrounded by four *şatîri*, two walking slightly ahead of the horse, and two on each side of the ruler, supporting his legs. Right behind the ruler, comes the *capuchehaia* or his envoy, and the convoy ends with the boyars of Moldavia, if any happen to be there, or some of the Greek nobles of Constantinople, family relatives, or friends of the ruler. With the convoy starting from the vizier's court, he exits the city through the Bahce-Kapu gate, formerly called *Chrysopyle*, and goes directly to the Fanar to the great church of the Patriarch of Constantinople. Whoever sees the ruler passing, no matter if they are Turks or Christians, even if they're sitting at work in their shop, has to stand up, cross their arms and bow their heads; if the convoy passes through the janissaries' gate, the guards on duty are aligned by their superiors until the ruler passes through, and they greet him in the same way they greet the vizier, lowering the hem of their garments (which for them is the greatest sign of respect which shows they honor their ruler so much, that they have to stand up in front of him covering their feet and unmoving unless he commands it) with their right hands on their chests and their heads bowed. Upon reaching the Patriarchal church with his convoy, the Turks are given the command to stop in the road, and the ruler enters the church courtyard on horseback, dismounts his horse near a boulder found there especially for this ceremony, while the ceaușii shout their usual cheer: *Hak teâlâ padișahumuze ve beg effendimüze çok yillar ömürler virsün, devlet ile çok yașa!*, which means "God the just and almighty give our Emperor and Voivode, our lord, long life, and may he live many joyful years!" At the outer gate that turns towards the road, he is greeted at the boulder, which I mentioned above, by the priest of *myrrh* of the Patriarchal church, the metropolitans, the bishops, and the rest of the clergy who happen to be there at that moment, and finally, when he reaches the church's doors, he is greeted by the

Patriarch who blesses him with the holy cross sign. While the Patriarch walks ahead and the cantors sing "he is worthy," the ruler enters the sanctuary, crosses himself in the middle of the church in front of the altar and, after kissing the holy icons, he walks toward the throne reserved for the ruler of Moldavia; after stepping over its threshold, the protodeacon recites τάς έκτενάς (the litanies) in which he also names the new ruler similarly: "Ἔτι δεόμεθα ὑπέρ τοῦ εὐσεβεστάτου γαληνοτάτου καί ὑψηλοτάτου αὐθεντός ὑμῶν Ν. Ν. κράτους, νίκης, διαυνής, ὑγείας σωτηρίας αὐτοῦ, καί τόν κύριον τόν Θεόν ἡμῶν ἐπί πλέον συνεργήσαί καί κατευοδώσαι αὐτόν ἐν πᾶσι, καί ὑποτάξαι ὑπό τούς πόδας αὐτοῦ πάντα ἐχθρόν καί πολέμιον", which means "we pray for the most pious, most brilliant, and with the highest authority given by the Lord, may he receive strength, success, stability, and salvation, and may our virtuous God help him lead, guide him in everything and subjugate under his feet every enemy and every adversary". After ἐκτενάς, the Patriarch dressed in his holy robes enters the altar together with four or more metropolitans where they are joined by the Prince, who kneels and rests his head on the edge of the *pristol*; the Patriarch covers it with his *omophorion* and after speaking the prayers that were once read during the coronation of emperors, anoints him with holy oil. After this, the ruler stands up and returns to his throne, while the cantors sing a certain polihron πολυχρόνιον, ποίησαι Κύριος ὁ Θεός τόν εὐσεβέστατον, γαληνότατον καί ὑψηλότατον ἡμῶν αὐθεντήν πάσης τέ Μολδοβλαχίας Κύριον Ν. Ν. Κύριε, φύλλαττε αὐτόν εἰς πολλά ἔτη. This means "God, give him long life to our most pious, most brilliant and holy ruler of all Moldo-Wallachia, and protect him for many years." Then the Patriarch also sits on his throne, and ordering silence, he makes a short speech about the merits of the ruler, urging him to keep the peace and defend the Church. The speech is followed by the *polihron* for the Patriarch, which almost always contains the same words and one for the ruler. Finally, after the ἀπολύσει (ending of the service), the ruler and the Patriarch come to the middle of the church, where the Patriarch strengthens him by blessing him with the holy cross, and the ruler, in turn, kisses the Patriarch's right hand. He follows the ruler out of the church, to the boulder mentioned above, where, after kissing each other, the ruler mounts his horse and is greeted out of the church's courtyard by the Turkish retinue, while the *ceauși* repeat the usual cheers, and they then return to the palace in the same order in which they came.

As soon as he arrives there, he only invites in the leaders of his companions, serves them coffee or other sugary treats, and gives them small gifts, after which they, together with their people, after wishing the new ruler good and joyful days, return to the vizier's court.

The next day, the Patriarch and the metropolitans come to greet the ruler and, after that, he is visited and congratulated by all the nobles of Greece that are in Constantinople. He is also congratulated by the envoys of kings from Christian countries, either themselves or their representatives, especially if they had connections in the past with the said ruler. In the following days, he is engaged in paying the sums of money owed for receiving the throne and with other gifts that Turks name *peșcheș* or goodwill gifts, but which in reality they extort from the ruler based on their insatiable greed. As soon as he pays half of them, he is sent the tokens of his reign, which consist of two horsetails (*tuiuri*) and a flag (which they call *sangeac*) with a festivity more pompous than the ones of the viziers who are honored with three *tuiuri*. Because they receive the tokens of their power from the *miralem-aga* (the one over the tokens) who sends them with no festivity; on the contrary, if they have to be given to rulers of Moldavia or Wallachia, they're taken through the whole city by a great escort, until they reach the ruler's residence. In truth, on the appointed day, the same *ceauși*, and servants of the vizier who escorted the ruler when he visited the church gather early in the morning at the *miralem-aga*, who's the keeper of the imperial flag, which is a high rank at court. After the Prince learns that all of them are gathered, he sends his envoys and the boyars, if any of them are there, dressed as exquisitely as possible, and especially with beautifully decorated horses, to the Bai-i-humaiun, which is the tallest gate, a name that represents the gate outside the imperial palace. At their arrival, the *miralem-aga* greets them with high honors and immediately calls for *tabulhanaua*, which is royal music arranged for the ruler. While the darabans, flutes, and other instruments that Turks use are being played, the convoy starts from the royal court in the following order: first come the *ceauși* in pairs, after them come pairs of the vizier's *agalari* dressed in the same clothing they use when in the Sultan's divan, next come the boyars together with the ruler's *chehaia*, after which, finally comes the *miralem-aga*, carrying the unfolded flag and two horsetails, and behind him come the musicians. While they go through the city, every guard, wherever they are positioned, even the ones at the vizier's court, are aligned in the street and, lowering the hem of their robes, with their arms crossed to their chests, must pay honor to the royal symbols. When they finally reach the Prince's residence, he, together with his courtiers, comes out before the flag bearer, welcoming him at the entrance of his palace, and the *miralem-aga*, bowing his head, gives him the flag and the horsetails, and speaks *Allah teâlâ mübarek eyleye* which means "May God bless you with luck." Taking the flag in his hands, the ruler kisses it respectfully and gives it to his *sangiacdar*, which means his flag bearer, after which he invites the *miralem-aga* in his receiving chamber and serves him, in the Turkish custom, with coffee and sweets, commands for him to be dressed in a sable-lined garment, and when he takes his leave, he gives him the usual tip. The *Miralem-aga* returns together with his retinue to the Emperor's court, but the *tabulhana* remains with the ruler, and every day, three hours before sunset (at the time the Turks call *ikindi*) plays, resounding cheerfully, the *neubet*, which is the sign of the watchers. Such an honor is only given to the rulers of Moldavia and Wallachia. Because no paşa, while residing behind the walls of Constantinople, is not allowed to play military music.

After dealing with his affairs at court and paying the sum of money he was imposed, the Prince only then sends word to the vizier through chehaia, that nothing prevents him any longer from assuming the throne and he asks him to facilitate a meeting with the Emperor so that he can ask permission to leave.

On the day appointed for this ceremony, which can only be on a Sunday or a Tuesday, because these were declared by Suleiman for the Sultan's divan, the Grand Vizier, the *muftiu* and the *cadiascheri*, along with the other viziers, *ieniceri-agasî*, *silihtar-agasî*, and others who can get in through their ranks, gather before sunrise and listen to the complaints of the folk, while the Emperor stays hidden behind gold grates. This trial is sometimes prolonged until the fourth hour of the day when nobody has any complaint left to make. After the divan ends, the Prince, together with his boyars, is ordered to wait in line from the arch of the entrance of the receiving chamber, to the furthest arch in the room, called the *cubbe*, after which the Grand

Vizier stands up and walks over to the Emperor, followed by the other viziers and the *cadiascheri*; when he passes through, the ruler greets him by bowing his head and treats the other viziers the same. As soon as they reach the Emperor, the Grand Vizier informs the Sultan of the affairs that were discussed in the divan or of other problems that concern the state, after which he informs him that his servant, the ruler of Moldavia, asks for permission to go to his country. If the Emperor allows it, the *capugilar-chehaiasî*, the head of the doorkeepers as he is called, shares with the ruler the Sultan's will and *muhzur-agasî*, the lieutenant of the janissaries aside from the vizier, orders for the ruler's head to be adorned with a *cuca*, which is a bunch of ostrich feathers, made with mastery. This adornment set on the heads of the rulers is worn especially by the janissaries, and it shows they are part of their clan, which is the reason why nobody else could set it on his head, aside from the *muhzur-aga*, who as long he is the commander of the guards at the vizier's court, is considered to hold the place of the entire janissary corp. After the ruler is adorned as such, the great *tefterdar* dresses him in a caftan and shares with the boyars 27 other caftans of lower value. Following this, two *capugi-başi* introduce the Prince, together with four great boyars, if they happen to be there, holding him by his underarms. As soon as he enters the receiving room, they make him bow his head to the ground, a gesture that is repeated after the third and the sixth step, and finally, when he reaches the middle of the room, he stops standing straight, because the room itself is not too spacious. The Emperor then turns from his *său taht* or throne towards the vizier who is standing to his right with his hands crossed, and instructs him what to tell the Prince; first bowing to the ground in front of the Sultan, the vizier addressed the ruler with the following words: "*Senün sadakatun ve istikametün izar-ı haziret padişah-ı âlempenah effendi müzurî olmakle, sena Boğdan voyvodeligin ihsan buyurdılar. Imdi sen dahi sedakat ve istikamet ile hidmet-i padişahîde bul unup ve ferman meta şeriflerine itaat ve inkıyat ve riaya-ı saymakdur ve dikkati mevfur eyleyesin; illâ sen bilürsin ki taksiratıne bir vechile cevabe kadir olamazsin*" which means "Because your faith and your honor were made known to our master, the Emperor, the salvation of the whole world, being gracious to you, gave you the throne of Moldavia. Therefore, you are also indebted to him from now on to serve him with faith from your heart, being obedient to his most holy commands to which the whole land must obey, and fulfill them with the same devotion: to the joyful subjects of our commander and Emperor you must protect and show mercy, find out with care and diligence everything our enemies plan, and send reliable news in every moment, and this you must do using all your strengths and means. Otherwise, you know (without a doubt) what awaits you. And if you do wrongs, you will not be able to exonerate yourself giving groundless answers." At this, the Prince, if he spoke Turkish, answered shortly on his own: *Adaletlü ve merhametlü padişahımun hidmeti aliyelerinde var kudretimi sarf eylemek can u baş üzre, heman nazar-ı âyin-i hümayunleri bu âciz bendelerinün üzerindendür eylemeyeler*, which means: "I promise with my soul and head (or everything I regard more than my head and my life) to put all my strength in the service of the most just and most merciful Emperor, but may he not turn his merciful and benevolent gaze away from this humble and insignificant servant (from this worthless slave)." and saying this, walking backward (because showing your back to the Sultan is not permitted) he is removed from the room by the *capugi-başi*, with the same ceremonies as when he was received. Meanwhile, the *buiuc-*

imbrohor (the head of the royal stables), waits at the middle gate holding an Arabian horse with reigns shining of gold and precious stones, covered with a Phrygian-crafted *shabrack* in gold and silver; from its saddle hangs his sword on the left and his topuz (mace) on the right. Two *iedeccii* (servants of the royal horse) hold the horse, while next to them stand two *acchiulahlîi* (servants with white caps on their heads) and two *paici*, runners dressed in garments embroidered with gold thread, each wearing on their head a silver headdress in the shape of a big cup (known as a *mitre*). There, the mounted Prince waits for the vizier and orders his boyars to line up on his left; he then greets the Grand Vizier when he passes him and also greets the other viziers by bowing his head and bringing his hands to his chest, at which they respond by nodding their heads.

After they return to their palaces, the ruler leaves court with his retinue and with the military music, with the *paici* and the royal *acchiulahlîi*, and goes straight to the Patriarchal church where he is greeted by the Patriarch and the clergy with the same ceremonies and honors that I mentioned above. At the entrance, he removes his *cuca* and does not put it back until he leaves.

From there he goes straight to his palace, where he is taken to his receiving chamber by the same *alagari* that accompanied him. They, after receiving the usual gifts, return to court, and the *paici* and *acchiulahlîi* remain by his side and accompany him to Iași, the city of the princely throne. The next day, the *Reis-Effendi*, the grand chancellor of the Ottoman Empire, sends him a diploma written in golden letters with beautiful features and commands him to return to his country as soon as possible. All this is because the ruler is not allowed to stay in Constantinople for more than a week after meeting the Sultan. On departure, the Emperor gives him an *iskemne-agasî* as a traveling companion, which is the one assigned to seat the ruler on his throne. This mission is given to one of the more intimate servants of the court: the *kapugilar-chehaiasî* (the great doorkeeper), the first or the second *miriahor* (the ones over the royal stables), and not rarely even the *silihtar* or *ciohodar*, which have the highest ranks among servants; however, because of their many and difficult duties, do not accompany the ruler themselves but send others to do it in their stead. Aside from this, a *capugi-başa* is ordered to accompany him, together with four ordinary *capugi* and as many *ceauși*, two *acchiulahlîi*, two *șatîri,* and two imperial *paici*, as well as the same *tabulhana* or musicians that the vizier normally has.

After everything is in order, a day before leaving Constantinople, the ruler asks for permission to say goodbye to the vizier, and after he receives it he goes to the vizier's gate together with his representatives and a few boyars. At arrival, the *chehaia* takes him to the vizier's chamber. The vizier advises him to be faithful, repeats the earlier conditions, and lets him know of others that he would find helpful in certain circumstances. At this, the Prince replies according to the situation, invokes the vizier's kindness for him and his representatives, and kisses his hand. After all this, the vizier permits him to leave, and usually gives him good wishes in the following manner: *Göreyim seni; var sağliğ ile! Allah teâlâ işini âsân eyleye!* Which means "I'll see you! Behave like a man and be brave. Farewell with health and may God ease your task." He then commands him to be dressed in the garment they call *izn-caftan*, which is a sign of farewell. After the ceremony ends, he meets *chehaia* in his chamber and takes his goodbyes for the last time, after which he finally mounts his horse and either returns to his palace or visits the other viziers. This is normally done during the night more than during the day so that the ruler doesn't give the impression that he has other protectors at court. The next day, with a convoy and as great a festivity as possible, he leaves the capital, walking slowly, cheered by the *ceauși* who, as I said above, start every time the ruler mounts or dismounts. At the head of his convoy are Moldavian riders, if the ruler has any by his side, carrying his flag ahead. They are followed by Christian music, *darabans*, and trumpets, and behind it, a white flag, a symbol of peace and submission; in the middle are the two *tuiuri* or horsetails, which were given to the ruler at court. They're followed by the ruler's *capuchehaias* and the boyars found in Constantinople, surrounded on both sides by a row of *ceauși*. After them, come the horses decorated with blankets and *harșale* embroidered by Phrygian craftsmen; around them are six of the ruler's *șatîri*, and behind them two royal *șatîri*. After them comes the ruler on horseback, wearing a royal garment and *cuca*; the head of his horse is shaded by two of the Sultan's *paici*, and two *iedecci* or horse servants hold his stirrups. A little behind them, on the ruler's left side, the side that by Turkish standards is more honorable, stands the *ischemne-agasî*, and on the right, the *sangiac-agasî*, the keeper of the flag. Behind the ruler come his housekeepers, and after them come three red unfolded flags, from which the middle one has half a moon on top, or *alem*, and the others are adorned only with golden spheres, worn by the ones who hold the place of the *sangiac-agasî*. After them comes the *tabulhana* with a bigger *daraban* making a deafening trumpet sound. At the end of the convoy come the house servants of the *ischemne-agasî*, of *sangiac-agasî*, and other ordinary people that have to accompany their masters.

In this order, as I said above, they reach the first stop, which is not far from the capital's walls. For the rest of the journey, they don't respect the ceremonies that closely, but every time they reach a city or a village they must respect the usual cheers from the *ceauși*, the music, or the other ceremonies. Each time during the journey, two *ceauși,* together with a servant of the ruler must go ahead to reach the next stop, which they call *conac*, and deal with accommodations and food; all these are done according to the ruler's wish. In truth, because of imperial command, all must obey the Prince in everything like he was the Grand Vizier, and even if one of the Turks was insolent or wouldn't want to obey the ruler's commands, he could be punished with the deserved punishment through the ruler's *beșli-agasî*, but if he wanted to be more merciful, he could give him to his superiors to be punished.

Reaching Galați in this manner, the first city of Moldavia when coming from Constantinople, they are greeted by all the boyars of lower Moldavia and the ones from upper Moldavia that live close by. Accompanied by them, he starts towards Iași and on the way, he inquires about the situation of the inhabitants, listening to their complaints, and judging their causes. A mile from Iași, he is greeted by the *caimacami*, or their representatives, people that were set in rank by him from the time that he was still in Constantinople, together with the other boyars, soldiers, and townspeople that he receives to kiss his hand and robe. He then enters the city with the same festivity as when he left Constantinople, and close to the great church named after St. Nicholas, dismounts his horse. At the entrance, the Metropolitan, together with the other priests, bows at his coming and invites him into the church, where they perform the same ceremonies as they were done in ancient times, as I showed above. After the ἀπολύσει, while he leaves the church, he is received by the Turkish retinue, that during this time waited in the road, with their usual cheers and music. With the same companions, he heads towards the palace, and as soon as he gets there he is introduced to the Grand Divan, as it's called, facing the *iskemne-agasî,* and stops in front of the throne with three steps that is found there. After the boyars take their seats, the other heads of the army are invited to the divan, together with the richest merchants of Iași. Finally, silence is ordered and the *iskemne-agasî* gives the divan's secretary, usually called *divan-effendesi* (who is Turkish and in the service of the ruler for a high salary) the royal decree, *hiucm ferman,* which is his ruling decree. This is written in similar wording:

"You, the highest ones among boyars and most outstanding people of the country, bishops, leaders of Moldavia, riding hosts, infantry, and all my subjects and servants, may your end be joyful. By the time the almighty command of our brilliant imperial majesty reached you, whom all the land obeys, take note that in such and such year, such and such month, our infinite kindness, taking into account the faith and honest works of the chosen one from the people that believe in Jesus and of the greatest boyars of the Nazars, he considered him kind and worthy of our mercy, kindness, and help. This is why we indulged him, adorned him, and gifted him with the reign of Moldavia. But to the same, we harshly commanded to take fatherly care of the boyars of all ranks, of the higher-ups set at the helm of other realms, and of all his subjects, to defend and help them, to obey our commands without question and serve us with faith and honor. We command you to be obedient and humble in all and fulfill with zeal and without delay everything he will charge you with at our command. And whoever will be even a little disrespectful and stubborn and won't want to obey his orders, whatever rank he was, to punish his malice and stubbornness with his sword or whatever else punishment, or fine, however, he considers, to condemn him and hit him. Therefore, you must acknowledge the one named above as your sovereign and ruler chosen by us and set at your helm; beware of having any thoughts or working cunningly against him, and have faith in our holy signature (the inscription above the name of the Emperor) and that's what you should know. Given at Constantinople in such and such year, such and such month."

After reading this firman by the *divan-effendisi* and the dragoman translates every sentence, all boyars reply in one voice, all together: "may the royal command be done." Then *iskemne-agasî* dresses the ruler in the caftan he brought with him and supporting him with the right hand, sits him on the throne; at this moment the cannons are fired and the *ceauși* shout their usual cheers. After he is secured on the throne in this way, the ruler orders that *iskemne-agasî* be gifted a coat lined with sable fur, and *divan-effendisi* and the Great Postelnic with the usual caftan. At the end of these ceremonies, the high Metropolitan wishes him luck and abundance in a short speech and kisses his hand, which the ruler also does in turn after the Metropolitan blesses him. After the Metropolitan, the bishops and first rank boyars come to kiss the ruler's hand and robe, whose names the *Great Postelnic* speaks out loud, adding the words: "Your Majesty's servant, such and such, kisses your righteous robe." The postelic does the same thing with the second-rank boyars and the third-rank boyars.

The boyars are followed by the heads of the army: the *chiliarhi*, captains, *sutași* and their representatives, and also the merchants and other important townsfolk of Iași.

After this, the ruler retreats to the back chamber, and *iskemne-agasî* is led with a great escort, having the great gatekeeper ahead, to the host that was decided for him.

The next day the boyars gather again in the Grand Divan, where after taking the seats they had before, comes the ruler preceded by the group of *postelinici* and passes from the great hall to the one usually named the small *spătărie*.[40] There, after the ruler sits on the throne, the seven ranks of Moldavia are called one by one, by the postelnic of their rank. And when each comes in turn, the ruler either removes him from his rank, strengthens his rank, or promotes them from one rank to a higher one; but to lower one's rank he's prevented by the country's customs (unless someone doesn't follow this), otherwise, he can decide whatever he wishes regarding them like he wouldn't know of anyone above him on the face of the earth. After deciding everything according to his will and dealing with the leadership of the country given to him, allows the *iskemne-agasî* and the other royal subjects to return to Constantinople, loaded with many gifts, and accompanies them with all the boyars for a distance of a thousand steps outside the city; he then tells one of the boyars to accompany them to Galați, while he returns to Iași.

---

[40] *Author's Note:* It is usually called so, because the ruler's sword is always set on the table in that chamber, and nobody else enters it aside from the seven first-rank boyars.

Chapter IV
About the Acknowledgment of the Ruler

In the way I showed you now, the beautiful scepters are entrusted to the ruler of Moldavia by the Ottoman Court, but they're so easily broken and if they're not secured with very hard circles, they're dropped out of one's hands easier than you'd speak a word. Actually, from the way the Turks usually behave with the Moldavian people, they showed that not unjustly it is said about them the proverb "hunt rabbits not with dogs, but with the cart" and that they don't have the habit of luring a horse without having something in the bag. Of course, they considered it better to tame with lures the wild Moldavian aurochs, whose fierceness they tried, not once, and not without losses, than to appease his fury by force, hoping a day would come when he would cast aside his past fury and, losing his strength because of blood loss, would endure chains and shackles out of need.

For this purpose, when Bogdan III, son of Stephen the Great, was the first to subjugate the country to the Ottoman Empire, he was refused no honor, and the laws of the country, the civil and religious ones were acknowledged, the supreme rule was allowed to keep its symbols and Turks were satisfied with being acknowledged as vassals and required to be paid four thousand gold coins yearly. After Bogdan's death, a greater honor was given to his son, Stephen IV, which the boyars chose as their ruler and lawfully set in power, and he was sent the keeper of the royal stables, as an envoy by the Sultan, to congratulate him for taking the power and to bring him the usual tokens, the tui, sangiac, royal cuca and a royal horse beautifully decorated. To his heirs, even if higher tributes were imposed on them, the Turks didn't dare to refuse any honor or to disturb the voting process, until in the time of John, called the Armenian, they found the opportunity to step over the old privileges and impose heavier burdens on the country, unknown until that time. After they caught John, the one named above, plotting a rebellion, and breaking their promise, had him killed, they started to subdue Moldavia in tighter chains and asked that if the ruler of Moldavia doesn't want to be considered an enemy, he must obtain a confirmation of his reign from the Ottoman Court every three years. Nothing that an outworn Moldavia can't refuse this condition, later, under Miron Barnovski's rule, the Turks imposed another condition through which it was commanded that the ruler was to receive his tokens in person at court, to come by himself to the Grand Porte every three years and bow to his Emperor. For this to be done more eagerly, after that the rulers were changed and removed from power more often, and they became so afraid, that they started looking forward to being summoned to court after the second or the third year, and to receive the Emperor's kindness and the confirmation of their reign, but especially, being afraid of the vizier's greed, they ask the confirmation by themselves. This is given to the ruler easily if the vizier doesn't suspect anything about his faith, or if another didn't offer more money, and then the vizier sends the following *talhîș* to the Sultan: "Because Moldavia's current ruler, that showed himself faithful to the Ottoman Empire for so many years and didn't hesitate to put neither his life nor his fortune in the empire's service, and above that sent the entire usual tribute to the Porte, because aside from this he led the boyars and the rest of the population of Moldavia with such kindness and justice, that they begged you in repeated letters and witnessed they're happy under his rule and ask Your Majesty to please strengthen his rule, and I consider him worthy of your mercy, and for everything else I await Your Majesty's high command."

This letter is presented to the Emperor in the usual manner of Turks by the talhîşci (letter bearer) and after the Sultan signs it with the usual wording *Amel oluna*, meaning "it will be done according to the report", is brought back to the vizier by the same talhîşi. But the vizier, although he obtained the Sultan's confirmation of the rule, however, to extort more money, pretends nothing was obtained from the Sultan regarding this matter, even chehaia, the vizier's cunning tool, summons the ruler's representatives, lies to them telling them that because of the conspiracies of some and secret whispers of the court's servants, the Sultan is harder to convince than expected; his master, the vizier, he adds, reminded the Emperor a few times about that problem, but he still didn't receive any favorable reply.

Finding out about the true or made-up danger in which their ruler is, the representatives throw themselves at the chehaia's feet and ask him to support their ruler's interests in any way he can, and finally, they increase the sum of promised gifts for him and the vizier. Therefore, ambition and greed race to mock the poor Moldavians, until they satisfy their unmeasured pride and their desire to have as much as possible from the courts they have in their subordination. Finally, after they all agree on everything and chehaia realizes he can't extort more, he lets them leave hopeful for a good favorable outcome; the next day he lets the representatives know, through one of the vizier's

About the Acknowledgment of the Ruler

servants, who doesn't fail to return with empty hands, that the vizier finally obtained from the Sultan the permission for their ruler to be strengthened in his rule, and he summons them to court. When arriving there, they're first taken to see the chehaia and then the vizier himself, and after hearing from his own mouth of the Emperor's mercy towards their ruler, they're dressed in caftan as is the custom. A few days later, the vizier sends *capugilar-chehaiasî* to the ruler, or another that he prefers from the imperial servants, and asks him to deliver the new reign firman, as well as the ruling command, simply named *hiucm-ferman*. The firman is usually the same as the one given to the ruler at the start of his reign, but the conclusion, instead of being *Voydelige tevcih olunmak ihsan-ı hümayun olmışdur*, meaning "You're gifted with the rule through kindness and goodwill," it's written *Voydeligine teedid ve mukarrer olunmak ihsan-ı hümayun olmışdur*, meaning "Your rule is renewed and strengthened through mercy, etc." And the command sound almost like this: "Highest among rulers of the people who believe in Jesus and most blessed among the elders of the Nazarenes, ruler of Moldavia of today, such and such named. When our command would have reached you, you must acknowledge that after finding out about your undeniable services and deeply searching your faith in us, we considered you completely worthy of our mercy and goodwill and because of this, we ordered your reign of Moldavia to be strengthened and renewed. Therefore, we gave you complete rule and power over Moldavians, the subjects of our majesty's; to them, you must share justice, like you have done before, the boyars and all the people of Moldavia of any rank you must protect and defend and not hesitate to inform our brilliant Porte of every need, oppression, and pressure they might have, without delay. Aside from these, you must be ready to fulfill our majesty's commands that will be sent to you, and putting the bottom of your robes to your waist[41] you must use all your power for them; you must send on the decided date to our treasury the whole annual *haraci* that was decided for Moldavia.

Beware of thinking or doing anything else and believe in our holy signature. Given at Constantinople, in the year... month...."

This command is accompanied by a letter from the vizier, through which he informs the ruler that, though his requests and interventions, he finally obtained the strengthening of his reign from the unmeasured royal mercy.

Armed with this letter the *capugi-başa* travels to Iași with long haul horses, usually called *menzil* horses and when he reaches Galați, sending an envoy ahead of him, notifies the ruler of his arrival and the day he will enter Iași. On that day, the ruler together with the whole court greets the *capugi-başa* one thousand steps outside the city; as soon as they meet, they greet one another on horseback, and congratulate each other; after that, the ruler returns to the city with *capugi-başa* on his right, which in Turkish culture is the place of lower honor. Ahead of them walks a servant of *capugi-başa*, holding the royal firman wrapped in white fabric, and in his arms, the caftan prepared for the ruler; behind them comes the royal music and the ceauși, that shout on and off their usual cheers.

In this order, they travel to court, where, after the ruler together with all the boyars enter the Grand Divan, and he sits on his throne, the *capugi-başa* gives him the firman and the ruler gives him the

---

[41]*Author's Note:* Expression from Turkish that shows readiness and zeal to serve someone.

divan-effendisi to read. All this is done in the order I described above at the choosing of the rulers.

Aside from the strengthening of the reign, which is usually done once every three years and is usually called the "big mucarer," another is done every year, called the "small mucarer," which requires lower expenses than the big one, and about which we'll talk more below. At that time the firman is not renewed, but only a *hiuc-ferman* is sent, or a command from the empire, this being sent through a middle-rank subject of the vizier and this is especially why it has to be rewarded with smaller gifts.

Chapter V
About the Removal of Rulers from the Throne

After we discussed the election and confirmation of Moldavia's rulers, I believe a curious reader is somehow entitled to ask me to talk about their removal from the throne. I'll do my best to keep the same order I followed before and search more closely, from the documents I have at my disposal, the way of their removal in the past and today. Of course, in the first centuries, after Moldavia was founded, the rulers were not removed and could not be removed. Because they led their subjects according to their will, just like kings, and they earned this power more through ancestry, then through choosing; our chronicles say however that a few times the rulers of the Moldavian nation were banished from their reign because of internal discords, not through an act of force from the outside. Besides, Moldavia did not acknowledge the right of primogeniture, which cures European kingdoms of the wounds caused by internal disagreements, and again the laws of the country forbade the reign to be shared; it was the parent's decision which of their sons they wanted as heir, through their testament.

Every time the unexpected death of a ruler prevented this from happening, or if the brother's ambition disturbed the process, it wasn't possible to avoid internal fights for power. Through these the

About the Removal of Rulers from the Throne

one with the most luck at war grabbed the reign; the one defeated, if he was able to run retreated either to Transylvania or to Poland (lands in which many rulers had their ancestors) and there they were waiting for the right opportunity to gather their strength and up their game. This made the historians of Poland and Hungary generally conclude, using particular cases, that Moldavia's rulers were their vassals and are obliged to apply the nationality names to the rights resulting from friendship. Aside from these, it happened a few times that the ruler, either because of his tyranny or because of an evil deed through which he hurt the boyars, was removed from the throne through the boyars' scheming, and sometimes even killed. Besides these ways, there was no other way for rulers to lose the crown, but the one that once took the scepter kept it until his death, without anyone's resistance. This rule was first dismissed with Peter V, named Rareş, the natural son of Stephen the Great, who Suleiman I, the Turkish Emperor, banished from his reign, accusing him of burning Chilia, and set Stephen VII in his stead, who was at least alive, who claimed that he was the great-grandson of Alexander I. The second time this happened was with Peter VI, named Şchiopul, who, even if he was chosen by boyars after John the Armernian's terrible death, the Turks then removed him, still shortly after, regretting their decision, gave him back the rule.

Though quite rare, the Turks used force with the rulers and not even then, unless it was a face-to-face confrontation, until taking Moldavia's right to vote after Miron Barnovski betrayed them, gave the scepter to their liking to Ilie III, the son of Alexander IV.

Since then nobody, apart from Eustratie Dabija and our father Constantine Cantemir, got to end their days on the throne. Whoever wishes to research this more closely, please consult the list of Moldavia's rulers, given by us in Chapter II.

And the removal from the throne of Moldavia's rulers is done today in the following way. As soon as the vizier decides to banish Moldavia's ruler from the throne and receives by talhîş the leave to do so from the Sultan, he keeps his plans most secret, not telling anyone about this, except the new ruler he named, so that the representatives of the one who needs to be removed to not find out about it and not to inform him.

Then the vizier's chehaia summons the new ruler during the night in changed clothes, commands him to choose *caimacami*, meaning deputies, and to order them aboout what they need to do according to the imperial ordinance.

These being planned, the vizier chooses a *capugi-başa*, who's ordered to take the decree to the ruler and to bring him to Constantinople. The new ruler gives him a companion from among his servants, entrusting him with letters and ordinances for the *caimacami* he chose and for all the boyars of the country. Then the same *capugi-başa* is provided with two imperial decrees, from which one is addressed to the ruler set to be removed, and the other to the *caimacami* chosen by the new ruler. The content of the first ordinance, assigned to the ruler is usually the following: "Highest among rulers of Messiah's people, all glorious among the nation's greatest or congregation of Jesus (because removed rulers are adorned with the same honorific titles as they had during their reign), which you were before Moldavia's ruler, may your end be joyful. When the ordinance from our brilliant imperial majesty, to which the whole land submits, would have reached you, you must know that through your laziness in fulfilling duties and through your negligence in executing the orders given by our imperial majesty, you became guilty of all sorts of punishments and condemnations (sometimes even the death penalty is added). But, because of the kindness and pity, our majesty feels towards you, we only decreed that your reign be taken away and given to such and such named.

For this reason, you must come quickly at the entrance of the Porte of our brilliant majesty, together with your whole family, with your servants and treasures you might have, without delaying an hour or a second. Beware of thinking or doing things another way and have faith in our holy signature. Written in the year… month…."

The second ordinance addressed to the *caimacami* is usually written in these words: "The chosen ones from the greatest among Messiah's people, such and such named (because usually two or three caimacami are named and each name has to be mentioned), may your end be joyful. When the present ordinance of our imperial majesty would have reached you, you must know that we were notified that your present ruler, such and such named, shows himself lazy in fulfilling our orders, doesn't accomplish his duties towards us, doesn't take care of the good of his people and country, neither does he protect our subjects how he should, by being just and merciful to them; on the contrary, he oppressed them and extorts them in various ways.

For this reason, our infinite kindness sourced from the pity we feel towards you, he decreed that the one named above be removed and taken to the brilliant Porte. That's why you must obey our decision, give the named ruler to the *capugi-bașa*, remove him from the throne together with his whole family, all servants, and all his fortune, but beware of anyone treating him with disrespect, or daring to take something from his fortune. Afterward, everything your new ruler, such and such named, will impose upon you at our command, you must obey completely, without excuse; beware of thinking or doing things another way and have faith in our holy signature. Given...."

If the Turks had any fears that the ruler, finding out he's fated to become a simple person, might rebel or run to the Christian princes in the neighboring countries, they sent other ordinances to the *seraschier* in Babadag or the one in Bender and commanded them to put at the disposal of *capugi-bașa* a group of soldiers which could help them catch the ruler and send him to Constantinople under a strong guard. If everything seems calm and no motive arises for which the ruler might want to abandon his fortunes, the *capugi-bașa* by himself, provided with the two ordinances I showed you above, starts his travel towards Iași as soon as possible with a long haul horses, the ones they call *menzil*. On the way, especially when he reaches Galați, the first city of Moldavia that borders Thracia, he hides the reasons for his mission and, to lure the ruler who is not expecting him, spreads the word that he is there to deliver a completely different ordinance. Finally, he decides his departure in such a way, so that he reaches Iași before noon when all the boyars are gathered in the divan. He then starts towards the royal palace, enters the divan, greets all the boyars gathered there, and gives the imperial ordinance to the *caimacami* chosen by the new ruler, the ones that the servant that accompanies the *capugi-bașa*, dressed in Turkish clothing points at, speaking the following: "Your ruler is replaced, you must listen to the imperial commands and the ones of your new ruler." The servant of the new ruler also greets them in his name, the one in Turkish clothes that accompanies the *capugi-bașa*, and gives them the letters his master entrusted him with. Finally, after all the boyars gathered in the great hall, the *capugi-bașa* follows them, who the ruler must greet at the entrance of the hall. After they bow to each other, the *capugi-başa* commands him to get on the throne, because he has some things to communicate to him, from the order of the Emperor. Even though the ruler can easily guess what's happening from everything unfolding around him or that he's being deposed, still he listens, takes his seat, and humbly adds: "may the order of the kindest and glorious Emperor be done". After this, the *capugi-başa* hands him the imperial decree; the ruler, after he kisses it and takes it to his lips and forehead as is the custom, gives it to his *divan-effendisi* to read; while he reads it aloud, the ruler, *capugi-başa* and all the boyars listen standing up. At the end of the reading, the *capugi-başa* takes the ruler from under his arms, but respectfully, and orders him, after stepping off the throne, to sit in a smaller chair. Then the ruler, facing the *capugi-başa*, addresses him saying that he infinitely owes the kindest Emperor for not wanting to lose his unworthy servant, but to right him through a gentle scolding and that he receives with a light heart everything that his majesty would have decided for him; he also adds that he's aware of his guilt, and he won't lose his hope for the Emperor's kindness and everything he considers would win the favor of the great Turks. Then, after the ruler ends his speech, the *capugi-başa* leaves him with the boyars for three days and orders them to ready carriages as soon as possible, and everything necessary for travel; speaking this he returns to his host, chosen by the *caimacami*, and the ruler retreats to his palace. There he remains for three days after his deposition was announced and during this time, he keeps the ruling power he had before, to give orders and forbid whatever he wishes. All the boyars give him the same respect which they gave while he sat on the throne, and if any of them dared to be disrespectful towards him or touch his honor with any word, he can smash their bones with the mace or the *topuz* he received from the Sultan when he was named, without anyone resisting; even if he pierced a first rank boyar with his sword, as long as is done by his hand, the Emperor can't blame him in any way. Because Turks say in a proverb of theirs that the stone once used for a building, cannot be disregarded as a building stone and that a time will come when it will be needed again when building a house.

Also, during these three days, the servants chosen by the *caimacami* to accompany the ruler, get the horses ready, the carriages, and everything needed for travel. After all is done, the ruler exits through the small gate of the fortress, the one looking south, yet in a carriage, not on horseback, with his retinue, family, and fortune, from which nobody dares, at least not while he's present, to steal or to keep something worth an obol, and starts towards Constantinople. All the boyars and all army commanders accompany him for a mile and there they dismount and kiss his hand, bowing like he still had the rule of the country, in a sign of goodbye; in turn, the ruler thanks them for the respect they showed him and for the companionship he had with them and advises them, as political customs dictate, to obey the Emperor's orders and those of the new ruler. Following this, the boyars return to Iași, but they give him two companions to handle his accommodations and necessary food. During the journey, the *capugi-bașa* is careful not to allow the deposed ruler to meet with the new one on the way, and if this happens, the new one must step aside and let the other pass freely.

After he crosses the Danube, he's allowed to send some of his servants ahead to Constantinople to meet the vizier and whatever friends he has there, to convince the leaders of the Ottoman Empire to be more benevolent towards their master. If they can satisfy their greed with gifts, they get an ordinance for the *capugi-başa* to take him to his palace; if this ordinance cannot be obtained, when the *capugi-başa* arrives near the city, he stops and sends word to the chehaia through one of his men, that he brought the ruler and now is waiting for the vizier to tell him what to do with him. But if the ruler is accused of more serious wrongdoings, or if the Turks want to extort more money, he's ordered to be kept under guard. This guard, if they want to be more lenient with him, is done at the *capugi-başa's* residence or that of the *baş-bakyculi*, the public money collector. If the Emperor appears angry with him, he's taken to the seven towers, because nobody can be imprisoned there, unless they have an express and precise order from the Emperor. But whatever kind of guard he was kept under, it would be difficult to reclaim his freedom if he didn't redeem it with a nice sum of money and large gifts. Once freed, he lives at leisure in his residence, waiting for an opportunity to take the throne again. Finally, even if he's deposed, still, when he listens to the holy service in the Patriarchal church, he sits in the royal pew, in which nobody can sit aside from the patriarchs found in Constantinople. His wife enjoys the same privilege, having a special pew of her own, higher than the others in the narthex of the church. Aside from this, the ruler builds his house according to his will, decorates it as beautifully as he wants, and has connections to the envoys of European, French, English, Belgian, and Venetian princes, because Turks believe someone living in Constantinople can't plot something against the Ottoman court. He walks through the city together with four or more companions, the horse he rides is decorated as luxurious as he wants it to be and his servants wear whatever color they wish, even though in the past a Christian was forbidden to wear green garments or yellow shoes. Every time he visits the vizier, he dismounts at the doorstep, is greeted even by the chehaia and others with ruling titles, he's offered coffee and sweets, and he's shown all the respect that Turks usually show to a ruler on the throne. In times past, the dethroned rulers and the rulers' sons were given a pension of five or ten imperials a day, given from the imperial coffers, but this custom was later abandoned. However, even today, the ruler and all his servants are exempted from paying taxes and can openly bring in wine for the needs of his court, but he can't sell it. But the rulers didn't even wish to sell it because any type of trade, aside from the selling of produce they grow on their own land, is considered among Moldavians as being despised or inappropriate among nobles.

He considers himself lucky even the ruler whose disposal from the reign is not due to any fault of his own, but due to the vizier's greed; in truth, because the viziers are changed often after the Turkish customs, the successor, to reveal the deceptions and the greed of his predecessor, first searches the sum of money unlawfully extorted over that originally decided on from the rulers of Moldavia and Wallachia. That's why, to make his guilt even worse, he often washes away the blame from the ruler, who isn't that blameless to begin with, and accuses the other one of being greedy, in order to ease his way towards the riches he must collect.

Chapter VI
About the Boyars of Moldavia and their Ranks

Because until now I mentioned the boyars of Moldavia many times and I will do it even more often in the next chapters, I consider it appropriate to tell the interested reader about their duties and ranks in detail.

The name of "boyars" given to them by the natives, is Slavic and seems to have originated from the word "Boliare," a word through which, after an old custom, the Slavic nations used to name their elders; the Latin barons, was given not by the authority of the old, but by the use practiced in the neighboring courts. Their origin is unsure and because of the negligence of the first historiographers of Moldavia, is covered in darkness; however, the examples we have from the neighboring nations, the Serbians and the Bulgarians, prove these habits are older than the founding of Moldavia, although the old rulers of Moldavia didn't use to share the governance of the court with the nobles in an identical manner. In our old chronicles it is said that these ranks of leadership, that persist today, were established by Alexander I, named "cel Bun" (the Good), after he obtained from John Palaiologos the title of despot and the royal crown, and that he organized the whole court after the laws of the imperial court.

Whoever carefully compared the administration from the old imperial courts of Greece, which Curopalates and Georgius Codinus described in a certain book, with the ranks of the boyars from today in Moldavia, would easily believe what is told (by the chroniclers). For he will find from one or the other the same names, same duties, and same tasks of assisting the ruler, giving him advice and fulfilling them, helping him deal with public assignments, and dealing with everything related to the needs of the court and its dignity. That's why, the same way it was in times past in Greece, stays the same in Moldavia today, the boyars being split into council boyars or advisers and divan boyars, which you could call assessors. The council boyars, which are the ones who advise the ruler on matters related to the country, are the following seven:

1. The *Great Logofăt*, which you could rightfully call the supreme chancellor of the reign; he surpasses all the rest through honor and rank and is the president and the leader of all councils. First, he proposes to the other advisers what the ruler orders to be discussed, and after he gathers everyone's opinions, he informs the ruler what was decided; then, if he needs to ask something from the ruler in the name of all the other boyars, he is the one to reveal his wishes to the rest, while they sit quietly; this is the reason he received the Greek name *logothetes*.

Besides all these, he has the right to define the borders and judge the complaints about land possessions, as well as their services; at the same time, he's the courtiers' leader, meaning the same nobles whose ancestry didn't yet reach the rank of boyar. As a token of his rank, he wears a big sphere hung by his neck with a gold chain and holds a staff in his hand. While Moldavia was still flourishing, this rank was given the rule of Moncastru, which today is called Akkerman; however, after the Turkish army stole it from Moldavia, the *Great Logofăt* was given the rule of Cernăuți land.

2. The *Vornic* of the Lower Country, leader of inferior Moldavia, untangles all the problems of that province at the royal court, presides over all trials in that region, listens to complaints and judges them, can punish the ones guilty of murder, the thieves, the killers, the church robbers, and other knaves of this kind, even without the ruler's knowledge; as a sign of power, he wears a golden staff. During the old time, when Bessarabia was still part of Moldavia, and Chilia was under his rule before this city was taken away from the Moldavians, he was given the administration of Bârlad, where, because of his functions and the needs of the province required him to be at court at all times, he had two vornici of lower rank take his place.

3. The *Vornic* of the Upper Country, the leader of superior Moldavia, has the same rights in his province as the leader of lower Moldavia, and he holds as a symbol of his power the same golden staff. He's charged especially with the administration of the lands of Dorohoi.

4. The *Hatman* is the commander of the army, a function that during the old times of Greek emperors was held by the court's marshal. He's the head of all riders, meaning the soldiers on horseback, and has under his command paid soldiers, riders, as well as infantrymen. The ruler gave him the administration of Suceava, and he holds a golden staff.

5. The *Great Postelnic*, the country's most important official, deals with everything related to the matters of the court, has under

his command every courtier inside, and above all that he is the chief of military couriers to Constantinople and Crimea, usually called *beşlii*. In fact, he doesn't have a seat or the right to speak in the council, however, he is often called upon, either from the others' decision or from the ruler's command; in this case, he is somewhat the ruler's representative and makes sure the other counselors decide as quickly as possible the solutions related to the country's needs, according to the ruler's will. Besides these duties, he also keeps the administration of Iași and administers justice to the townspeople. As a symbol of his rank, he holds a silver staff.

6. The *Great Spătar*, the bearer of the ruler's sword, leads the servants working in the *spătărie* and handles the administration of half the land of Cernăuți. During important celebrations, called royal celebrations, he wears a garment sewn with gold thread and adorned with a cap inlaid with precious stones; while the ruler attends the holy service at church and, while he sits at the table, he usually holds his sword.

7. The *Great Păharnic* (*supremus pincerna*) hands the ruler the first cup of wine during feasts and has the other *paharnici* under his leadership. He takes care of all the ruler's vineyards, orders for them to be worked and for grapes to be harvested at the right time, and he's at the helm of all the ones working the vineyard from all across Moldavia. No person in the whole country is allowed to harvest grapes, not even from their own vineyard unless he gives them permission for it, permission he normally gives on September 14th, after receiving a small gift. Besides, he also handles the administration of the lands of Cotnari. Among these boyars there is also:

8. The *Vistier* or the Great Treasurer. He collects the country's income and uses it according to the ruler's command. He keeps track

of all earnings and spending and all the treasury's secretaries, usually called "treasury *dieci*," who listen to his word. Also, he carries the key from the room where the council normally gathers, this being the only reason why he has the eighth place among the advisers, although, when he's among them he has no seat and no right to speak. Even so, if anything related to money is discussed, usually he takes part in the discussion, not to give his opinion, but to acknowledge everyone else's decision and execute it.

After these eight council boyars, there are the divan boyars, which are divided into three categories. The ones in the first class, whose members are called high boyars (*barones magni*), are in the lead.

The *Great Stolnic* is the one overseeing feasts. He's at the helm of the ruler's entire kitchen and all its staff. During feast days or if a greater solemnity takes place, he arranges the dishes on the ruler's table, is the first to taste the food, and remains standing up at the table until the third glass is served. Aside from other earnings, he's also given provisions from the ruler's personal kitchen.

The *Great Comis* is the one overseeing the stables and supervising all the stalls with horses that the ruler owns, the tools and their servants, the blacksmiths, and craftsmen while they make carts; he rules the Braniște, a very large pasture alongside Prut River, deals with scything the hay for the royal court's needs, from which he's given a certain share. Besides this, he obtains from the watermills on Prut River, which are many, a tribute of twenty imperials a year.

The *Great Medelnicer* pours water for the ruler to wash his hands during important solemnities and before eating and owns half of the lands of Ștefănești.

The *Great Clucer*, who you could call the steward of provisions, oversees all the ruler's pantries, in which are kept fruits, butter, honey, cheese, salt, and others, and in this way, he makes sure they are purchased in time and stored properly and then takes them out every time they are needed or the ruler asks for them. As payment, rulers gave them a tenth of the produce from the sheepfolds that peasants keep in the mountains of Moldavia.

The *Serdar*, a field commander (*campidux*), in the European speech called a general lieutenant, commands the riders from the lands of Lăpușna, Orhei, and Soroca and defends the territory between Prut, Dniester, and Bessarabia against Tartar invasions from Crimea and from Bugeac.

The *Great Sulger* or the highest among the butchers deals with gathering the cattle meant for slaughter, for the ruler's and courtiers' meals, and distributes the meat to those that require daily servings, among which is the *seimen* infantry.

The *Great Jitnicier*, chief of provisions, is the one that collects the wheat from all over the country for the ruler's needs and stores it in the court's granary.

The *Great Pitar* oversees the bakers and makes sure the flour is ready and fresh bread is baked daily for both the ruler and the ones that have a daily allowance.

The *Great Șetrar* handles the ruler's tents, and during expeditions, he oversees the war cannons and the other firearms and sets the camping place up, holding at the same time the function of artillery commander as well as the function of chief over the setup of camps.

The *Great Armaș* leads the other armed military men or the lictors, almost sixty of them; if anyone had to be tortured, he is in charge of executing the ruler's command; aside from all these, he supervises dungeons and military music, called *tabulhana*.

The second *logofăt* replaces the *Great Logofăt* or chancellor and is sent by him if he is prevented by more important duties, at delimitations of field or estate borders.

The *Great Uşar* is above all the other doorkeepers and handles duties related to the *capugi-başa* sent by the vizier from the imperial court and other imperial envoys.

The *Aga* supervises the guards of Iaşi, commands the *seimeni*, who in return for being exempted from taxes serve the military without pay, judges smaller complaints among the townsfolk of Iaşi, punishes any obscene or drunk man he catches on the street, whatever rank he was, having duties similar to the janissaries' aga from the Turkish court.

The second *postelnic*, in the *Great Postelnic's* absence, acts in his stead and supervises the entire court. However, his most important duty is to take to the ruler all the first-rank boyars removed from their positions and every second-rank subject, or if anyone has anything to ask, present the ruler with their requests and take the replies back to them.

The third *logofăt*, or the secretary, strengthens the ruler's personal letters with the small seal, writes them, and takes them to the ruler to sign them. He's the highest among the *uricari* or the certificate scribes and over the office, resolves monastery problems, brings the Metropolitan, the bishops, and the clergy to the ruler, and if any envoys arrive from other princes he makes sure the court ceremonies are respected, that usually happens at their arrival, also called audience. He wears a seal hung by his neck on a silver chain, which he normally uses to seal the judgment decisions of the *Great Logofăt*, written in his handwriting.

Captain of the *darabani* is the commander of the *darabani*, a name derived from the Germanic word *trabant*, an infantry army that guards the royal court; he checks the guards day and night, sets them, changes them, and if the *aga* is not at court, he also handles his duties.

All the boyars named above are considered to be first class and are called high boyars; aside from their rank, they enjoy the privilege of listening to the complaints of their subjects and judging them, all over Moldavia, wherever they happened to be, a privilege that second and third-class boyars don't have. The *serdar*, the second and third *logofăt*, the second *postelnic*, and also the captain of the *darabani*, even though they are in the same class as some high boyars who they receive orders from, would seem more appropriate to be mentioned among the next class, however, because their jobs are more honorable than the others, and they have to be close to the ruler daily, they earned their place among the high boyars and have privileges equal to theirs.

Aside from these, the next ones are considered to belong to the same class:

The *Vameș* (officer of customs), oversees the border customs and the căminar, who collects taxes owed to the ruler. Neither of them has a seat in the divan, having to stay where the ruler commands them. However, they can't get higher than the *serdar*.

After them, the next ones are considered to be part of the second class:

About the Boyars of Moldavia and their Ranks

The second *spătar* holds the ruler's sword during festivities of lower importance, and if the *Great Spătar* is not present, he handles all his duties.

The second *paharnic* also handles all the duties of the *Great Paharnic* in his absence, and he especially takes care of the ruler's vineyards at Huși where he makes sure to see them worked and harvested at the right time.

The second *vistier* keeps track, after the third *vistier*, of the registers with earnings and spending of the treasury for a trimester and informs the *Great Vistier*, order which is respected for every job related to earnings and spending.

The second *stolnic* leads the kitchen daily, orders what dishes should be cooked for the ruler then serves them at the ruler's table and tastes them first.

The second *comis* keeps the place of the *Great Comis*, takes care daily of the royal stables and if the ruler wishes to go riding, he gets his horse ready. A third of his earnings are in the form of food.

The second *medelnicer*,

The second *clucer*,

The second *sulger*,

The second *jidnicer*,

The second *pitar*,

The second *șetrar:*

They all fulfill their duties in the same order as the second *vistier* for a trimester, after the ones of third-rank.

The second *armaș* keeps the registers with everyone who's imprisoned and the ones that have to be executed, shows them to the ruler every Saturday, asks what he should do with the newly caught ones, and finally, he's sent with a few other *armași* to bring the offenders to him, so he can judge their guilt.

The second *ușar* usually fulfills the duties of the *Great Ușar* in his absence.

The boyars of the third class are the following ones:

The third *postelnic* has to be at court day and night together with two other postelnici of inferior rank. Their duty is that, if the ruler has something to command to the *Great Postelnic*, they must take the orders, also they are charged with other royal duties, communicated to them through the *cămărași*, duties that must be executed, and the outcome reported to the ruler; for this reason, these three have free entrance even in the *Great Divan*, a privilege that other boyars don't have.

The third *spătar* holds the ruler's sword daily and that's why, aside from his rank, has his own place among the court's servants.

The third *păharnic* handles the vineyards of Bacău and Trotuș and makes sure the vineyard workers harvest the grapes on time.

The third *vistier* is under the *Great Vistier's* command, and he is given the same work. After the *Great Vistier* makes records of the costs for three months, he gives their administration to the third *vistier*, who works on them for a whole month, after which this duty is passed to the second *vistier*, who after three months, as I said above, gives the administration back to the third one, after which he gives the records back to the *Great Vistier* after 30 days.

Thus, the administration of the public treasury passes continuously between the three treasures, so that the two higher ones supervise it for three months each, while the lower-ranked one is given this task for two months. This order is respected for the other jobs that deal with money, as we'll see below.

The third *comnis* has the same duties as the second one.

The third *sulger* and third *jitnicer* fulfill their duties in the same order, every four months, the duties of their colleagues with the same name from the higher ranks, just like the third *vistier*.

The third *cămăraș* shares the meat and weighs it.

The granary *cămăraș* keeps the records and accounts for the provisions deposited in the ruler's granary and receives a payment of 30 aspri for every cart.

The four gate *vornici*, have their seats outside of court, where they judge complaints of lesser importance, punish indecent women, and if any girl made a mistake with a scoundrel or if her honor was taken by force, they command for them to be married by a priest, as the religious customs dictate, if both of them are part of the townsfolk; and if one of them is of noble birth, it's reported to the ruler. Then they sit by the ruler's side during trials, command the people to be silent and bring the accused in the divan; if any of them promise by giving their word that on the decided date they'll come to the ruler together with the claimant, they note down this day in their records and whoever doesn't come at the appointed time is considered guilty through this disobedience towards their ruler. For these jobs, they are awarded incomes from the lands of Roman.

All the boyars I listed so far are provided for by the country and are used for royal services. That's why only the ones born in noble families rise to these ranks, even though the ruler has the freedom to give them to whomever he pleases, even to the lowest-ranked people.

When their wives come to the ruler's wife's chamber, which is somewhat like a *gineceu* (Greek-style royal apartment) to greet her, they sit on chairs in the same order that their husbands sit in theirs. But the ruler, besides the boyars listed above that deal with problems on the outside, also has servants that deal with tasks at court, usually named boiernași, who can be put in this category not only with the boyars, but with war hostages and housekeepers, and through this, they receive boyar privileges.

These are:

The *Great Cămăraș*. He supervises the Grand Divan's employees and guards the private coffers of the ruler, which is different from the country's treasury. He commands the pantry courtiers, the lower ranked boyars, sets the weights and measures the merchants must sell their goods at, watches to make sure they don't cheat the scales by pushing them with their elbows and if any are caught cheating, are punished according to the laws. Under his command are also the șarhorodeni merchants, which are the ones that bring goods to Moldavia from Kazakhstan and Russia.

The *vătaf* of the *divan's* pages is the one that supervises the pages working in the *divan*, and has almost the same function in Moldavia as the *ceauș-bașa* has at the Ottoman court. He's the highest among the pages of the divan and makes sure everything the ruler ordered during trials, whatever is unjustly taken or justly owed to another to be returned, and keeps a silver knife in his hand, as a sign of his duty.

The *vătaf* of the *stolnics* (stolnic's subordinates) is the highest among servants dealing with the ruler's meals, and when they bring the food to the table from the kitchen, he walks in front of them, with a knife in his hand, which is not made out of silver this time.

About the Boyars of Moldavia and their Ranks

The *vătaf* of the *păhărnics* (cup bearers) is the one supervising and commanding the cupbearers, which are the ones that usually fill up the cups at the ruler's table or during feasts that boyars attend.

The *cupar* is the one that daily administers the court's wine cellars; he gives appropriate amounts to innkeepers that sell wine, batches marked by the royal seal, and if anyone is caught selling wine at a smaller measure than the one established by him, he punishes them according to the law.

The *ciohodar* deals with the making of boots and shoes for the ruler and the rest of the court, and he makes the ruler's boots himself; all the shoemakers from Iași are under his command.

The *medelnicieri*, three or four in number, lay out the ruler's table daily, pour his water to wash his hands, and keep the bowls, plates, cups, and other things needed for feasts, the silverware and also the table covers, napkins and everything else that is needed at the table.

The inside *cămăraș* deals with all the clothes, gemstones, and other jewelry the ruler has, and commands the servants of the small chamber.

The *vătaf* of the *spătărie*, the highest among servants in the *spătărie* and *divan*, supervises them and gets his earnings from their work. Because these are often sent to the boyars, who the ruler summons from their villages, and if the boyar gives the servant, as the custom dictates, six gold coins as a gift, the vătaf gets one imperial out of them.

The *cămăraș* of jams, the one over sweets, makes sure the ruler gets on his table sweets and sugared fruits and keeps the porcelain dishes.

The *cămăraș* of shelves has under his care the saddles, the golden and silver reigns, and the rest of everything found in the royal stables.

The *pivnicer*, the one over the servants working in the wine cellar, is under the *cupar's* or *paharnic's* command, and he has in his subordination the ones crafting barrels or the others working in the cellars. He's paid in wine yeast from which he makes brandy.

The treasury *logofăt*, which is the treasury's secretary, commands all treasury clerks and keeps the spending registers while listening to the *Great Vistier*.

The register *cămăraș* keeps all the registers with the ruler's personal earnings, he also keeps the lists of soldiers and if the army makes a calling he calls each one by his name. This is how is also done when wages are paid, each captain receives a list with the soldiers' names from his group and for this work, he gets one imperial as payment from each captain.

The *cămăraș* of lights is the keeper of candles, collects the taxes in wax and fat, which is called *bezmăn*, and from it he supervises the making of candles and rush lights needed for the court.

The market *vornic* supervises the markets and collects the tithe from all the merchandise sold in markets by piece or by measure, which in Moldavia is called *mortasipia*. He then receives from the *cămăraș* of lights the candles and shares them among the courtiers. He's also charged with procuring firewood for the needs of the court and with sharing it in time for each chamber and kitchen.

The *vătaf* over the market pages is their supervisor, who collects the taxes and other payments from townsfolk and sends them over to the treasury. All these, together with their superior, are under the *Great Vistier's* command.

About the Boyars of Moldavia and their Ranks

The *paici's vătaf*, the highest among the *paici*, has under his command eight of the ruler's house guards, named *paici*, who wear silver girdles, silver swords, and spears with gold on their handles and tips.

Serving the ruler's wife are:

Two *vornici* who also command the land of Vaslui, a *comnis* that takes care of the stables, horses, and her carriages, and two *cluceri* who are charged with provisions and pastures for the court's servants and for the stables.

They are followed in rank by noble-born servants of the ruler, that through their jobs are groomed to have their ranks elevated.

The divan *cămăraşi*, fifty of them, keep close to the ruler when he's in the divan and are used to summon the boyars.

The *spătărie cămăraşi*, twenty-four of them.

The Grand Divan *cămăraşi*, twelve.

The *Small Divan cămăraşi*, three.

Seven postelnici of higher rank and twenty-four or more, according to the ruler's will, of lower rank.

The *divan* pages, fifty in number, whose jobs correspond to the *ceauşi's* job from the Turkish court, are charged with bringing the culprits who don't show up to trial on the appointed date, and with forcing the ones that owe money to pay.

Twenty-four *păhărnics* assist the ruler at the table and give him and his guests their cups.

Twenty-four *stolnics* bring all sorts of foods from the kitchen to the ruler's table.

Sixty *armăşi* are used to catch thieves, boyars that are planning to flee the country, or others accused of worse things.

The *uşări* are the ones who take to their accommodations the Turkish emissaries sent from the Ottoman Porte or the Tatars from Crimea, procure their food, and provide them with whatever they need.

Chapter VII
About the Army of Moldavia

After I showed you the names of Moldavia's boyars and of the court's servants, we'll talk next about the army Moldavia once had, and the one in charge today.

The country's chronicles say that the army of Moldavia, which used to be free, numbered 70,000, and sometimes even 100,000 soldiers.

Whoever thinks of how strong the neighboring countries Moldavia used to go to war against are (Turks, Kazakhs, Polish, Hungarians, people of Wallachia), and that contrary to their attempts, not only did Moldavia defend its freedom until the time of Bogdan III, but it also extended its borders, will easily be convinced of this. But if the power of the Moldavian people reached its peak during the reign of Stephen the Great, it started decreasing little by little. Because the first rulers after Bogdan III, who surrendered Moldavia to the Turks, because it was defended by them from the neighbors' attacks, stopped attending to the army, like anyone else who is enjoying the peace and considering it wasn't necessary to care for so many people for no reason, slowly left the army to lose its former bravery and diminish in size. However, the chroniclers of Moldavia say that until the time of Movileşi, not less than 40.000 soldiers were recruited, but after that, because of internal discords as well as because of Turkish deception, who were trying to take away the Moldavian Crown's shine, finding opportunity in rebellions, the power of Moldavia diminished so much that now they can only defend themselves against enemies with 6000 to 8000 soldiers. They are divided between paid soldiers, who are employed for a fixed price, and soldiers that do the service on their own money, receiving in return an exemption from taxes. The commanders of the paid army are:

Bașbuluc-bașa: he commands ten *buluc-bași* or captains, from which each has around 100 *seimeni* under his command. In Turkish *seimeni* mean soldiers who are hired on good pay, among which there are Serbians, Bulgarians, Albanians, and Greeks, for the ruler's personal guard, and who are always at court changing shifts, even their residences are around the city walls.

Four German captains, that in times past used to command a thousand soldiers each, now have barely twenty-five soldiers under their flag.

Four Kazakh captains that used to also command a thousand soldiers each, now barely command forty or fifty men of their nation, usually from the Zaporozhian horde.

Twenty captains on horseback now command around a hundred soldiers each for three imperials a month. They are under the *Great Hatman's* command.

The captains of Lipcan Tartars (a name through which we understand those Scythians living in Lithuania and following the Islamic religion), are four or more, depending on the ruler's wish.

The *Beșli-aga* are under the command of two *beșli* captains. The *beșli* are Turks or Tatars who the ruler uses to avoid corruption among Turkish troops and punish the Turks if they behave inappropriately because among the Ottomans it is not permitted for a follower of Islam to be punished or whipped by a heathen, how they normally refer to Christians.

The commanders of the free army, the ones serving in return for tax exemptions, are:

Buluc-başi of fortresses, four or five in each city or market, depending on their size, Iași having ten, are commanded by the *aga*.

Eight captains of *daraban* commanders, who are all commanded by the *Great Daraban* commander, are also under the *aga's* command.

Nineteen captains of a thousand soldiers, also named *chiliarchs*, gathered from the nineteen lands of Moldavia. In the past, they counted in their units a thousand Moldavian centurions, but in our times the number dropped significantly. They used to be under the command of the *Great Vornici* of lower and upper Moldavia, however, all those troops are now under the *hatman's* command. From among them, the ones stationed on borders guard the mountain passes and water fords; the ones stationed inside the country, where nothing is to be feared from the enemies, are used as guards at the *hatman's* court, and they're sent wherever they're needed. They used to be called *husari*, but these troops are now called *hînsari*. The *hînsari* of today from lower and upper Moldavia, are under the command of the *vornic* from each region, and they don't serve the army, but keeping their old military name, they work the fields, which gave the proverb "From arms to hoeing" its origin.

In rank with them, I have to mention the group of hunters of Moldavia, who together with the *Great Vătaf*, their leader, occupy the mountain area of Moldavia, near Piatra market, a village consisting of around one hundred yards. During the war, they always had to follow the ruler's army; in times of peace, however, they do the hunting, and they either bring the animals alive to entertain the ruler, or kill them for his meals: stags, buffalo, sheep, as well as other forest animals. For their troubles, they're given gifts and a salary consisting of gunpowder and bullets.

The riders of Țarigrad or the couriers from Constantinople, fifty of them, together with the vătaf who is their superior, all speak Turkish well and if they're needed, they travel to Constantinople, and, for their service, they are exempted from taxes and receive twenty imperials a year.

The riders of Galați are the couriers of Galați that are under a certain's *vătaf's* command and have the same duties as the one from Constantinople, but they only receive ten imperials from the treasury, no matter where they're sent. They number almost fifty men.

The Hotin *îmblatori* (couriers), around fifty or more.

The Soroca *îmblatori* or the couriers from Soroca are chosen from the ones that speak Polish and Russian and are sent when the need arises to Poland and Russia. They all are under the vătaf's command or their superiors.

The *fustași* are the ones carrying spears, counting twenty-four. During times of peace, they guard the ladies' chambers and the court prison where are imprisoned the court's servants, punished for smaller offenses, they beat with rods the ones that have to be punished by the ruler's command. They surround the ruler holding their spears during parades or when he goes out for a walk, doing the same job during the war. They are commanded by a certain commander called the *vătaf* of *fustași*.

These are the troops that the country has to employ in its service for the ruler. If he, however, wants to employ more soldiers using his personal treasury, nobody can stop him, but it's very rare in our times for the ruler to want to increase his army, unless someone plots a revolt, because they consider it better to keep their treasures tucked away, than give them to unnecessary soldiers.

Chapter VIII
About Court Ceremonies during the Ruler's Outings and Feasts

After everything said above, I think I'll do something useful and pleasant for the curious reader, and I'll give you a short description of the festivities and orders usually respected when the ruler goes out, during royal feasts, and also during religious services.

Every time the ruler leaves the city to visit a church or a monastery or goes to war, he never leaves without great festivities and without being surrounded by multiple groups of soldiers. At the head of the convoy, there are several guides and scouts, chosen for this job from among the soldiers or riders. They're followed by the riders who carry the flags and the captains so that the groups of soldiers are spread out and able to be identified.

On both sides of the flags walk the centurions of each unit, making sure the soldiers are walking in the decided order and in a straight line. Behind them come other riders and the couriers together with their supervisors, after which come riding horses with two *tui* (horse-tails) ahead of them, which the Ottoman Porte gave the ruler as a token of his given power. Following them come the ruler's sons, and then the ruler in the middle of the convoy. On each of his sides walk the pages, whose clothing and jobs I described above; a little behind them, on the right, there are the *comiși*, the ones over the stables, and the vătafi that have in the subordination the court's servants. On the left comes the *Great Postelnic* together with the other postelnici. In the third row behind the ruler, walk the *buluc-bași* on both sides, the older they are, the closer they stay to the ruler. The first part of the convoy is guarded on both sides by the *seimeni*, or the paid soldiers, the *ceauși*, which we could call in a European tongue, corporals, making sure they all walk in unison.

Immediately behind the ruler comes the *spătar*, bearing the ruler's weapons; after that come the housekeepers, the ones called *cămărași*, *paharnici, ciohodari,* and *medelniceri*. The first row after them is held by the *vătaf of copies*, which is the superior of the housekeepers together with them, the second one is held by the *păhărnicei*, and the third by the *stolnicei*. They're followed by the *Great Sangeac*, or *alem*, and two other flags that were given to the ruler by the Emperor at the start of his reign; behind the flags come the *tabulhana*, the Turkish music, and behind it walk the armed soldiers.

After them, in the first line come the great boyars, then the second rank boyars, and in the third line come the third rank boyars, all mixed in with the ones that used to have those jobs, arranged by the ranks of the positions they used to have. The convoy ends with the boyars' servants, townsfolk, and merchants.

And when the ruler goes to war, behind them come the cannons under the command of the *Great Șetrar*, the captain of *darabani* with the armed soldiers and the cannon soldiers, and also everything they need for camps and the supplies; otherwise, all of them walk among the rest of the boyars, according to their ranks. The reader will understand this convoy easier if he looked at the picture.

After he reaches a church or a monastery in this order, the riders stop outside the churchyard while keeping their rows, and when the ruler passes through, they greet him by bowing their heads, while the infantry, as much as it fits, forms a circle in the churchyard. When the ruler reaches the doorway, he dismounts and the *ceauși* shout their usual cheer "may he live many years." Then the Metropolitan greets him with the holy cross, while the deacons swing their censers, and he gives him the Holy Bible to kiss. After that, with the Metropolitan and cantors ahead of him, singing "he is worthy," after he worshiped the holy icons, walks through the altar where only the ruler and the priests can enter, and in the middle of the church he crosses himself; from here he walks towards his throne and, after sitting on it, he greets the Metropolitan by nodding his head and then does the same to the boyars sitting in their pews.

Because I'm describing the court ceremonies, it's not without use to shortly describe the order of the pews in the church.

On the right of the pillar from the middle of the church is the royal pew, three steps high, surrounded by sculpted golden grates; the royal coat of arms adorns each of its sides, and a golden crown covers the top, under which rests the icon of the saint the ruler chose as its patron. In front of it, at the pillar on the left, is the other pew, for the ruler's sons, similar to the royal one, but only two steps high.

On the ruler's right sits the spătar, holding his swords on his shoulder and in his hand, on his left sits the postelnic, behind him to the left pillar, sit the postelnici in a row, holding their staffs; behind them are ordered according to their ranks the other servants of the court. On the ruler's right, towards the altar, sits the Metropolitan with a bishop, behind them in the back being the seats of the monks, abbots, and cantors. On the left, two bishops with priests from their diocese sit in the same order in front of the Metropolitan. The row of priests ends with the *Great Vistier*, who keeps the alms ready if it was brought from afar, a donation the ruler normally gives when he's anointed and to keep the peace and piety of the listeners; the second and third *logofăt* sit on the left, the first of them having the deal with the problems and clergy of the monasteries, and the second because he has to cut and share the alms cake after it gets blessed by the Metropolitan or another priest.

The right corner is held by the choir of Moldavian cantors, and the left by the Greek cantors, who sing religious songs in both languages. Behind the pews meant for the ruler's sons, the first rank boyars are aligned in a single long row, to the outer pillar, and behind them are the boyars removed from their duties, then the chiliarchs, the captains, and the rest of them, as many as can fit in the church.

Behind the royal pew, as far as the furthest pillar, which is on the right side of the back of the church, are aligned the wives of the boyars, behind their husbands. At the base of this back pillar sits the ruler's wife on a three-step high throne; if she has any daughters they sit between their mother and the boyars' wives. On her right sit her handmaids and the noble girls that serve her; on the left, her two *vornici* stop the crowd from getting too close. Finally, closest to the entrance of the church, sit the wives of boyars removed from duty, behind their husbands.

The church walls are lined with chairs for them; however, nobody dares to sit on them unless for night wakes when the priests read about the lives of saints or David's Psalms. Only the ruler might remain with his head covered in church, and he doesn't uncover it unless "*Sfinte Dumnezeule*" (God Almighty) is sung, when the Holy Bible is read, or when the priests recite the Creed of Niceea of the

Christian faith and the royal prayer, or the priests speak the words of God through which the holy communion was ordered. When they reach the hymn, the Metropolitan is the first to go to the altar to kiss the holy icons, and the ruler follows; when he leaves his pew, all the boyars stand up and bow to their ruler, who then returns to his place. After the service ends, the Metropolitan serves blessed bread to the ruler, his wife, sons, daughters, and all the boyars that are in function receive it from his hand, while he sits in his pew; finally, the third *logofăt* lets them taste the church cake (*coliva*).

After fulfilling this ceremony, the boyars leave ahead of the ruler and mounting their horses outside the churchyard, aligned depending on their ranks, with their heads bare, they bow them to their ruler when he passes through, then accompany him to court in the same order as I described above. There they leave their horses at the outer gate (because nobody is permitted to enter the inside courtyard on horseback) and standing up in the middle of the yard, each according to their rank, greet the ruler when he dismounts; after he climbs the steps, turning towards the boyars with his head bare, he greets them in turn, after which everyone returns to their homes.

On the days during which no solemnity is held, the ruler is served his lunch mostly in the small room, and sometimes in the great hall or the woman's hall. He always takes his meals with two high boyars, two boyars of lower rank, army captains and commanders, and sometimes even old soldiers, depending on how much place is left at the table. Nobody can join him for dinner unless they're related to him or become a favorite through flattery or pleasant conversation. The ruler's wife sometimes takes lunch with her husband, other times she orders to be brought lunch in the women's hall, where she is served by *cămăraşi, medelniceri,* and the *Great Paharnic,* and other noble girls she chooses from the daughters of nobles and boyars. If it's a festive day, the table is laid out in the small divan. The sounds of trumpets and *darabans* announce the food is ready; the *stolnicei*, under the *vătaf's* and second *stolnic's* command, receive the dishes from the kitchen and give them to the *Great Stolnic* to lay them down on the table.

When the ruler arrives, the Metropolitan speaks the usual prayers and blesses the food, while the *Great Medelnicer* pours the ruler water to wash his hands. After the ruler sat on his chair, everyone else does the same according to their ranks, but the advisers and first-rank boyars remain standing up, doing their jobs. First, the *Great Stolnic* tastes the food served for the ruler, and then, when the ruler goes to take the first bite of food, the cannons are fired and Christian and Turkish music starts playing. The *Great Paharnic* serves him the first glass after tasting the wine poured for himself in a smaller glass, an act called credință in the Moldavian dialect. Following that, the Metropolitan and bishops (following the laws imposed by Basil the Great) are not allowed to eat meat, and are served fish and cheese) together with all the boyars stand up and bow their heads to the ruler, who is drinking; they don't stand up anymore for the other drinks, but they always nod their heads respectfully, even if they were drunk. The high boyars stand up near the table until the third glass is served; after that, the *Great Spătar* gives the sword to the second one, the second *păharnic* fills up the glasses and the rest of the second-rank boyars do the jobs of their superiors. Then the ruler serves them all a plate of food from his own table, who, after kissing his hand, take it and set it in a nearby room, where a table is laid out just for them. The same honor is shown to those staying close to him, lower-ranked boyars, *buluc-bași*, and captains honored with the same ceremonies.

After they all ate and drank enough, they return to their duties at the royal table, making sure the *păhărnicei* keep feeling the boyars' glasses, the *stolnicei* keep bringing food and the *cămăraşi* keep changing the plates and everything is done how is supposed to be done.

Soldiers armed with maces stand at each side of the table (because the table is long, not wide), to guard the ruler. After a few glasses, when their heads heat up, the first big goblet is poured as a sign of thanks for the heavenly kindness and mercy, the second for the Emperor's health, not giving a specific name, because Moldavians think that, on one hand, somehow inappropriate to toast for the Turks, but on the other hand, very dangerous to give wishes of joy to Christian kings when they're drunk. The third goblet is toasted by the Metropolitan, who first speaks a few words for the ruler's health, and when his name is heard, the boyars suddenly stand up and line up in the middle of the divan according to their ranks. At the end of the speech, he blesses the ruler with the holy cross, while he takes it to his lips and the cannons are fired all around the palace, mixing in with the sound of music, sounds from which they can only hear echoes, because of the wide arches of the palace. After the ruler, the Metropolitan pours a silver goblet but doesn't leave his seat, only stands up; all the boyars, the ones sitting up and the ones standing up, drink in pairs from the goblets handed to them, and after kissing the ruler's hand, supported from their underarms by the postelic, they return to their seats. After pouring this goblet, more are being poured for his wife's, sons', and daughters' health, and for any other reason brought up by the context, or just from them being drunk. The ruler never stands up before the candlesticks are needed; after these are set on the table by the *Great Medelnicer*, all the guests stand up and greet their ruler. The sign of an ending feast is the napkin the ruler sets on the table; the *Great Postelnic*, noticing this sign, knocks on the floor with the silver staff he carries in his hand; hearing this, everyone that can stand, gets up suddenly, and the ones who are too drunk to stand are lifted by others. When the ruler stands up, the *medelnicer* pours water for him to wash his hands and brings him a towel to dry them, and the Metropolitan brinks him thanks; the ruler then crosses himself three times and turns towards the boyars with his head bare to take his farewells. When he turns his back to them, the servants and *cămăraşi* that are present grab whatever they can off the table, for they consider it an honor to eat something from the royal table. However, in order to avoid losing any silverware, they're forbidden to take anything out of the hall; or if a bigger group chooses to eat separately, they have to show the ones that guard the silverware all the cutlery and plates they receive, and return it all by number. The other boyars are led to their homes, accompanied by royal music. The next day everyone gathers in the great hall, and after kissing the ruler's hand they give thanks for what was offered to them and apologize for whatever they did while being drunk.

Chapter IX
About the Royal Hunts

If hunting beats is normally a great pleasure for all the princes of this earth, it was a very usual thing to do for the rulers of Moldavia. Aside from the fact that hunting sometimes looked like some sort of war and that a nation prone to war had to prefer it to other physical exercises, it has a special meaning to Moldavians, because it was believed it led to the founding their country. But because over time the rulers exaggerated with it and didn't leave enough for the peasants who lived in the forests, just enough to earn their food, this often caused revolts or mutinies. Aside from this, wiser men observed that the rulers too inclined towards hunting don't take care of their country, they leave the problems on their friends' shoulders and the time assigned to important tasks is spent completely on this type of entertainment. Their descendants, learning from these troubles, set a limit for this exercise, so the peasants wouldn't carry such a burden, and the rulers wouldn't be completely devoid of their fun. They decided on four[42] intervals in a year, precursory to the four fasting dates of the Oriental Church, during which

---

[42]*Author's Note:* Aside from these four usual hunts, the ruler can gather the people whenever he wants to chase the beasts (because as I showed above there's nobody in Moldavia who can impose laws or limits on his wishes), however, through this he would get a bad name and stain his reputation, which would be remembered even by his later descendants; he cannot even discard the possibility

the country's occupants of any station: boyars, soldiers, nobles, townsfolk, and merchants have to join the royal hunt. During these days a few thousand villagers are gathered from the neighboring villages, who are ordered to go into the forests and chase the beasts

The fields around the forests are filled with hunters, some surrounded by hounds, others setting traps, and they easily catch the prey scared by the villager's shouts. But to make the hunters more eager, the ruler set a prize for each animal: whoever catches a rabbit gets a bacşiş (because that's the Turkish name they use for this gift) of twenty-five aspri, whoever catches a fox gets sixty; the wild boar is rewarded with an imperial, the bear with a gold coin and the deer with eighty aspri. At the end of the hunt, the clean animals, the ones good to eat, are taken to the royal kitchen, others are shared among boyars or army superiors; the ones that cannot be eaten: foxes, wolves, bears, wild cats, dogs and other animals of this kind that live in the mountains of Moldavia are given to the pages or the ruler's servants, who earn good money from selling their pelts.

---

of being told on by the boyars at the Ottoman Porte of this oppression. That is why if sometimes lured in by the beauty of time or place, he wants a small pleasure, he organizes a hunt with his subjects and army who are always bound to follow him; however, this mustn't be done often enough to cause him to not pay attention to the needs of the country.

Chapter X

About Royal Funerals

The way all Moldavians give their ruler the greatest respect during his life, they give him the same honors when he dies. As soon as he passes, if it happens during summer, he is embalmed and kept in the palace until everyone gathers in Iași: every leader, boyar, bishop, archimandrite, and every abbot of every monastery, even monks, all the ones that are well known for their pious lives, and the highest of the priests. During this time, he's dressed in royal garments, adorned with his royal symbols, and subjects in high functions are praying at his side, together with the boyars and his servants, staying around him the same way they did when he was alive; the whole nation walks through the city with their heads bare to show they're mourning, and during the days in which the funeral is prepared, the bells toll day and night.

On the day decided for him to be taken to his grave, the same pompous festivities are prepared, as it was done during his outings when he was alive. At the head of the convoy walk the clerics, reading the usual funeral prayers read in the Oriental Church, surrounded on each side by troops, with their flags and arms pointing to the ground. All show their mourning through their expressions and clothing, they even make their horses look sad by making them tear up with onion juice. The first rank boyars carry the coffin on their shoulders, passing it along the way to the second rank boyars and to the last ones, to show in this way that they'll always be ready to obey their deceased ruler like they did while he was alive. The convoy ends with military music and *daraban* drums, which make a lamenting sound.

He's carried in this way until they reach the Metropolitan church, and until the religious service starts, he's set in front of the throne on which he sat while he was alive. After the service, the preacher stands behind the pulpit and has a long speech about the merits of the deceased, talks about his virtues, and shows the country what it lost because of his death; finally, he soothes the listeners for their loss and asks them to hope they'll know the same virtues from his son or successor. At the end of the speech, all the bishops, abbots, leaders, boyars, and everyone who was a subject of his court, walk to the coffin, kiss his right hand and the cross he holds in it. After they fulfill this last duty, if the ruler chose to be buried in the city, he is taken to the decided site, with the same festivities as when he was brought to the church, and he's lowered in the grave with silk ropes by the highest boyars. The first to throw dirt on his coffin is the Metropolitan; while he does it the cannons are fired and the tolling of the bells together with the sound of musical instruments makes a distressing noise that doesn't stop until the grave is filled. But if the ruler commanded to be buried at a monastery far from the city, a few boyars together with all the courtiers must accompany his remains there with great festivity; on the way, they must respect the same rules towards the deceased as they did when he was alive. Every time they pass through a town or a market they pull the coffin from the cart, put it on their shoulders, and carry it this way until they're out of the town; finally, when they reach the monastery chosen for burial, they take him to the grave site with the same ceremonies as the ones described above, his royal symbols being hung on the church walls and on the same wall being painted his face.

Chapter XI

About the Laws of Moldavia

We cannot know what were the old laws of Dacia, because the historians keep silent about these things; we can, however, assume by looking at the customs of the other barbarian nations, that the will of the ruler and the natural right had the power and authority of written law. After Decebal was defeated by the Emperor Ulpiu Trajan and the Dacian nation was eradicated, Dacia was converted to a Roman province and populated with Roman people, receiving Roman laws from its new settlers. They lasted in this country for as long as its people obeyed the Roman emperors and the ones from Constantinople; but after the invasions of the barbarian nations rid the country of its inhabitants, forcing the leaders of Constantinople to abandon the province and reinforce their own walls, the Roman laws started breaking down as well and changing so much for the inhabitants of Dacia, that when Moldavia was founded through Dragoș' joyful dare, the judges could hardly know what decisions they had to take. Seeing these shortcomings, Alexander I, Moldavia's despot, who our people named cel Bun (the Good) because of his great traits when he received his crown from the Emperor of Constantinople, adopted the Greek laws that were written in the τών Βασιλικών books (*Basilicale*), and making an extract of those extensive volumes, he introduced these laws that are now used in Moldavia. However, the various customs of the neighboring nations that they adopted through their wanderings and exiles, couldn't be erased completely from the life of this nation, because about all the nations of this earth have special customs when it comes to succession, testaments, sharing of the fortunes, land delimitations, and servitude.

Therefore, two types of rights were born in Moldavia from all this: a written law, which is based on the edicts given by Roman and Greek emperors and on the councils' decrees, and an unwritten one, which we could rightly call the "land's law," even though in usual speech is called *obicei* (custom) by Moldavians, which is a Slavic word that means tradition or use. But because those last customs didn't have a written foundation, and were often used differently than their true meaning by bought judges and brought injustice with them, Vasile Lupu (the Wolf), the ruler of Moldavia, gave a command during the last century through which good men that knew the law well, had to gather together all the country's written and unwritten laws, and composed a corpus that became the norm of a just sentence for Moldavia's judges and is still used today.

Chapter XII
About the Seat of Judgment of the Ruler and the Boyars

During the whole year, aside from the days the Church decided on for the great fasting, as it is called, the ruler judges public disagreements in the divan three or four days a week. And the divan, which is a Turkish word Moldavians use to describe the courtroom, is reserved for the middle room of the royal palace. There, a throne is set at the back of the room for the ruler, adorned on top with an icon of Jesus Christ coming before the court, which is always illuminated by a burning candle. On the left side, which according to Turkish customs is more honorable than the right one, is the Metropolitan's seat, after which are the boyars' seats, arranged according to their ranks; in front of the right wall sit the boyars removed from their functions. In the middle, on the ruler's right side sits the *spătar*, holding his sword, and a little further away sits the *Great Postelnic*, with a row of other *postelnici* by his side. The others, whose services are required in the divan, like pages and soldiers, stay further away from the ruler, but in his sight.

As soon as the ruler, who first prays to Christ the judge, sits on his throne, silence is commanded and from the number of litigants standing together at the door, two or three are introduced in the hall by pages, at the order of the *vornici*. After their claims are listened to, if they're not imprisoned, they're taken out of the divan through another door that opens to a small yard, while others come in turn, until none are left. As soon as the noon bell is heard, the rest of the crowd, if any are left, is rescheduled for another day. This judgment is so drastic and doesn't take into consideration the ranks, so much that even if the *Great Logofăt*, if someone complained of him, as soon as he heard his name he'd have to stand up and wait on the left side of the peasants until he's judged.

The more serious offenses are judged by the ruler himself, and the lighter ones are left for the boyars to judge. The boyars who are given this role, do it at their residence and give the sentence the way they feel fit. If both the claimant and the culprit are happy with it, the sentence has the same power as if it was given by the ruler. If one of the involved parties claims losses from the sentence, they can request judgment from the ruler himself. When the problem is analyzed again by him and if it's discovered the boyar's sentence was unfit, either because he was bribed by one of the parties, or because he was biased from the start, or because he simply doesn't know the law, he's punished severely. But if the ruler finds the judgment was served according to the law, whoever claimed it to be unfair is whipped for disobeying the boyar, gets his deserved punishment according to the ruler's will, for wasting the ruler's time, and is commanded to pay double the court costs for his adversary.

And if the ruler himself wants to judge more serious offenses or murders, he commands both the culprit and the claimant to be brought to the divan, and both are given the freedom to speak in their defense or to prove the guilt of the other one. After the debate, the Metropolitan and all the council boyars speak their opinions aloud, even knowing the ruler has another opinion, declaring the accused either guilty or not guilty. The boyars removed from duty are not given the right to speak or voice their opinions unless they're directly asked by the ruler. After everyone says whatever they need to say, if the culprit is found guilty, the ruler asks the Metropolitan what punishment would be fit for him according to civic and religious laws. The Metropolitan first reads the text of the law, then he asks the ruler for mercy, knowing nobody can impose anything on him, but the boyars still try to do it sometimes. Finally, the ruler gives the sentence, and he either forgives him or sentences him to die or to another punishment. Murderers are given to the *Great Armaș* to be imprisoned, and the ones imprisoned for debts are given to the *vătaf*. Punishments differ. Thieves are hanged, heretics are burned, killers, if they're boyars, are beheaded, and if they're peasants they have a slow and painful death, getting a stake through their ribs. These crimes rarely get any forgiveness from the ruler, maybe only if the killer comes to an agreement with the victim's relatives, and they declare in front of the ruler that they forgive him and don't want the blood to pay for blood, or to punish a death by another death. If the killer manages to obtain this forgiveness, he can hope for forgiveness from the ruler as well, but it's not sure he'll make it out alive. Because, if the ruler is convinced from his previous offenses that his malice can't be remedied through punishment, or there are other motives for which he believes he should be removed from among his people, he usually replies that his accusers and relatives of the victim can forgive the crime he committed, but he cannot stand for killers or villains to keep living among his people and defile their healthy members with his filth; taking this into account, he either punishes the criminals with death or with work in the prison.

If the boyars steal anything from the country's treasury for their own use, or if they plot any misdeed towards their ruler, which happens quite often because of Moldavians' volatile tempers, they can be punished by the ruler without consent from the other boyars, having to pay with their lives and their fortunes. If through delaying the sentence no harm would be done and if he doesn't fear the other schemers, he uses this necessary punishment as a virtue, to show everyone the justice of his decision and to bring horror to others that might do the same. He orders for the culprit to be brought in the divan, finds him guilty of treason, either by showing intercepted letters or through other evidence, and sentences him to die or to another punishment. However, if he's sentenced to death, he could only be executed by beheading, but if he needs to be beaten, only the ruler can do that using his mace, strikes that, even if they're very heavy, don't hurt their honor because it's considered very shameful to be whipped by others. The other troubles don't take too long to be judged, and more often than not the cause is judged and a sentence is given on the same day, or if it's more complicated, in three or four meetings. If the ruler is prevented by sickness or by other problems, he can't come to the divan, however, the boyars all gather in their seats and listen to the complaints of the people and judge them as if the ruler was there; the sentences with the summary of the complaints are sent to the ruler in writing. Finally, when the ruler goes to church or wherever else to take a stroll, anyone can stop him for a petition; the third *spătar* gathers all of them and sets them on the table for when the ruler returns to court. The third *logofăt* comes and reads them all to the ruler, writing on each one the decision; however, he shreds the ones which he considers to be an attempt to hide the truth.

About the Seat of Judgment of the Ruler and the Boyars

After that, the *spătar* returns all of them to the petitioners and the highest among pages makes sure the will of the ruler is fulfilled.

Nobody ever heard even a rumor that any ruler's justice was ever bought with gifts, or that he strayed from it out of favor, even if this was observed a few times with the boyars.

This is the custom in which matters of afflicted townsfolk are brought and judged in front of the supreme judge of Moldavia, meaning the ruler. Now I should talk a bit about lower-ranked judges. These have the right to judge everywhere, in the whole country, or at least in certain parts of it, which are the local judges. All the royal advisers, especially the great boyars of the divan are given the right to listen to complaints and judge them all across Moldavia, as soon as they leave the capital of Iași; the higher power, however, is given to the *vornici*. No resident of the lands under their lead can refuse to show up for their trials, however, if other boyars don't want to be judged by them, they can refuse it and request judgment from the ruler before a sentence is given. If the *vornic's* sentence didn't appease one or the other involved, they have the freedom to appeal to the ruler's judgment seat.

But when their troubles reach there, they're not widely discussed anymore, only if the sentence was given justly and according to the laws of the country, as is shown in the *vornic's* decision, which is normally handed to the winning party.

The same thing is done if someone makes an appeal to the ruler about the decision of a boyar if they get sentenced before they come to trial. If the sentence of the boyar proves to be unjust, which rarely happens, he usually gets a severe punishment. If it's proven that the sentence was justly given, and the person in question just gets pleasure from going to trials, the boyar's honor is considered to be slightly harmed, and the guilty person is whipped and made to pay all the court costs for the claimant. As a matter of fact, the first-rank boyars can listen and judge complaints even in Iași, of course, if both parties agree to it because, from the ruler's judgment seat, nobody can be turned away. However, when one of the boyars judges in the royal divan troubles that are assigned to him, he must present to the *Great Logofăt* through a scribe, the sentence given together with his reasons for it. If this is found just and according to civil or religious laws related to it, he writes in his handwriting underneath "it was searched" and gives it to the third *logofăt* to strengthen it with the divan's seal; through this it becomes final. However, if he believes the boyar gave an unjust sentence, he shreds the document and asks for the troubled parties in the royal *divan*. In truth, outside the royal court, not even the *Great Logofăt* can review or dismiss the sentence of another boyar, and a lower-rank boyar can never annul the sentence of one of superior rank.

Because the higher boyars must always be at court, and they can't judge matters throughout the whole country, to share justice among Moldavia's residents, each city or market was given certain judges, which in some parts of the country are called *pârcălabi*, and in other parts are called *vornici* or *cămărași*.

At Hotin, Cernăuți, Suceava, Neamț, and Soroca there are two *pârcălabi* that, because these are the greatest fortresses of Moldavia, are given the names of commanders; there are also two in Roman, Botoșani (a market that is under the ruler's wife's command), Orhei, Chișinău, Lăpușna, Fălcii, Galați, Tecuci, Tutova, and Putna. The other markets of lower importance, like Bacău, Târgul Frumos,

About the Seat of Judgment of the Ruler and the Boyars

Hîrlău, Covurlui, and Vaslui, each have just one *pârcălab*. Two *vornici*, which are deputies of the *Great Vornic* in lower Moldavia, share the justice in Bîrlad, same as many in Dorohoi, as deputies of the *Great Vornic* of upper Moldavia, two at Cîmpulung and one at Vaslui; over the salt mines around Ocna, there are two certain *cămăraşi*.

They can listen to every complaint, but can only judge the lesser offenses; the more serious ones they must send to the *Great Vornic* of their province, but if an appeal was made, to the ruler. This is done in the following way: the *pârcălab* writes a letter in which he says that because of such and such named, they kept opening law-suits for such and such issues, they made an appeal to the ruler and promised to show up on the decided date. He tears this letter in two and gives each involved party one half. If one of them doesn't show up on the decided date, they must pay the *ferîia*, which is a fine consisting of money: the peasant gives twenty-five gold coins, the boyar a hundred, and a high boyar six hundred. They can't give any excuse for not paying it unless one was prevented either by sickness or a duty made in service of the ruler or if he was charged with something by the country and his superiors.

Chapter XIII
About Moldavia's Income in Past and Present Times

The country's chronicles and the property titles of the rulers show better than anything that ever since Moldavia was founded by Dragoș, it's only been the ruler's patrimony.

Because the new residents of Moldavia couldn't choose their lands, they were given to them by the ruler if they proved themselves worthy through heroic acts, also receiving boyar ranks, villages, and lands to maintain their given titles. The truth of this is strongly shown by all the property titles of the old nations of Moldavia, on whose foundation the people of today own their properties, and they don't mention anything else, but the ruler's generosity. To illustrate this more, it would be better to quote here the property title given by Stephen the Great to our ancestor Teodor Cantemir; the words are somehow like this: "because Teodor Cantemir, the *pârcălab* of Chilia and Ismail, proved himself a loyal subject and a brave soldier of the cross in defending those citadels against Turkish and Tatar invasions, and because after that, with God's will, all these lands were abandoned and occupied by Turks, and he was forced to flee his ancestral lands through their advance, lands that his grandfathers and great-grandfathers received as gifts for their loyal services to our predecessors, we, urged by Christian love and duty, gift the above named Teodor

Cantemir with three villages in the lands of Făclii, and with them, all the forests, fields, rivers and springs that are part of them, and we give him the highest power over the Tigheci forest and name him supreme captain of Tigheceni riders (which according to historians of that time were about eight thousand)" etc. In the same way, are written the property titles of other families. This explains the fact that in Moldavia there are almost no boyar families to not get their names from the village they received as gifts from the ruler, the founder of those families. That's why Cantemir was then named Silișteanul, after the name of a village he owned, Racoviță after Racova, Ureche after Urechești, etc.

But, because with time the boyars' numbers grew significantly and these gifts seemed to swallow the country's income completely, the rulers divided the incomes that were gathered before for the country and the ruler's needs, so that the whole community would benefit from it. For the court's management, they kept all the towns and markets of Moldavia, together with the twelve nearest villages, the salt mines, tributes, and the tithe on sheep, pigs, and on beehives owned by peasants and lower-ranked boyars, because high-ranked boyars were always exempted from taxes. All the others were left in charge of the country and the boyars, and they decided that during times of peace, every peasant household must pay the usual *fumuri*, eighty aspri each, meaning one florin, if they're threatened by war, one imperial, meaning a hundred and twenty aspri, and if the great need arises, one gold coin each, which at that time was valued at two hundred aspri. The reader will be able to understand that from the great sum of money that was collected from everyone, forty thousand Moldavian soldiers could be paid, and the other fourteen thousand brought from afar: Germans, Kazakhs, Serbians, Bulgarians, Albanians, and Greeks. The ruler's income was over six hundred thousand imperials a year, and the public records show that only from Câmpulung the tithe gathered was of twenty-four thousand sheep. In our days, however, Moldavia is so poor and unhappy, that it only gets a sixth of the income of old.

It's true that from tributes and customs, they collect around thirty thousand imperials, ten thousand from the salt mines, fifteen thousand from towns and markets ruled by the *pârcălab*, usually ten thousand from the sheep tithe, but in the first year of reign, when the boyars are made to pay the tithe, twenty for the tithe on beehives and twenty-five for the tithe on pigs, fifteen thousand from the courtiers or the lower-ranked boyars; all these added together bring the income at around one hundred thousand imperials.

These earnings the ruler can use and spend to his will, for his needs and his court's needs; the limits of the country's treasury are decided, not by the subjects, but by the need and greed of Turks. They can't be refused anything, whatever they asked for, but the ruler can't be forced to spend his personal fortune on the country's needs either. The care of the entire public treasury is given to the seven high boyars, commonly named council boyars; only they can enter the treasury (the hall decided for discussions regarding the most important topics). The only one who is not a council boyar, but who can sit among them, is the *Great Vistiernic* because he is in charge of the treasury and carries its keys. Therefore, whenever a command comes from the Ottoman Porte or the ruler considers is for the good of the country, he asks through a written command that the seven boyars must meet and decide the matter at hand. They gather in the treasury hall and, after discussing among themselves, they send their advice to the ruler through the *vistiernic*. If their advice pleases the ruler, he orders the decision to be fulfilled within these many days. Then two or three people, even more, if it's required, are sent to collect money or provisions or whatever else they were asked to collect, and they give the *vistier* everything for which they receive written proof.

The *vistiernic* must inform the same seven council boyars about the earnings and spending of the past three months.

If times are peaceful, three or four hundred thousand imperials are collected in the treasury; however, if a new ruler is sent from the Porte or if the old ruler is strengthened in rank through a new firman, around five hundred thousand imperials must be collected; all this money is taken and extorted in various ways from the poor people, to satisfy the insatiable greed of the Ottoman Porte.

Because of them, the number of misfortunes and torments grows by the day and threatens the country with boundless devastation.

Chapter XIV
About the Tributes and Gifts that Moldavia Pays to the Ottoman Court

Ever since the Turkish armies lined up the banks of the Danube and until the time of Stephen the Great, the Moldavians defended their freedom heroically and couldn't be lured to put their necks under foreign occupation, not through enticement or great promises, neither through the example of the Wallachians, their neighbors. And things were like that even though the rulers of Moldavia, chronicles say, paid the Turks great sums of money a few times. Because softer rulers, whenever they could ransom the country from under oppression, rightly preferred, from the example of the wise illustrious leaders of the Venetian republic, to suffer losses from their own purses, rather than from their country and subjects; however, a steady and continuous tribute could never be imposed in the times of Stephen, named above.

Eventually, his son, Bogdan cel Orb (the Blind), gave Moldavia to the Turks, even though it was said that this went against his father's testament. The conditions were the following: he must give a yearly gift of forty thousand gold coins, forty horses, and twenty-four falcons, not as a tribute, but as a way to show submission to their power, and if the Sultan had to go to war, Moldavia had to send four thousand soldiers to the Turkish army, and to clear roads and repair bridges. These conditions lasted for nearly a century, and the Turks, happy with the fact they restrained the Moldavian bull, didn't dare to ask for more until they made sure it got used to it. However, following John the Armenian's rebellion, Moldavia's forces were weakened considerably, and the Turks started asking for a tribute (*haraci*) from his successor, Peter called Șchiopul (the Lame), consisting of nineteen thousand gold coins. Even though the boyars asked to be exempted from it, Peter didn't want to go down in history as the one who subjugated the country and that's why he abdicated and retreated to Transylvania, where he kept his fortunes. The ruler set in his stead by the Turks, Iancu Sasul, a very cruel and greedy man, a Sardanapal of Moldavia, gave everything to the Turks in return for his reign, and he wasn't afraid to soil his name, which he didn't even have before this.

Over the years, the rulers tried a few times to get rid of this oppression that came especially with internal discords, but the Turks found so many opportunities to increase the tribute that it was increased from twelve thousand gold coins to sixty-five thousand imperials given to the Ottoman treasury today. To take this tribute, if the Ottomans are busy going to war with other princes of Europe, each year they send to Moldavia one of the closest servants of the Emperor, with the title of *hasne-agasî*, which is the one in charge of the treasury. He's brought to the city by the ruler with great festivity, and after he counts the money, he gives them back to the ruler, ordering him to send them to Constantinople. For his troubles he receives from the ruler seven thousand five hundred imperials and a sable fur; as a matter of fact, he sometimes has to be given a bigger sum of money, if the vizier commands it through his letter, or if he's aware that the *hasne-agasî* has the Emperor's favor. After the ruler's representatives pay the tribute to the Emperor's treasury, they receive a written proof from the *hasne-agasî*, which is presented to the *maden-halfasi*, the one over the mines, who gives them another proof through which it's shown that this year's tribute was paid.

Both documents are brought to the *mectupci-effendi*, the first secretary of the Grand Vizier or his intimate secretary, who, after receiving the proof from everyone else, gives another proof for the money being paid.

When the *capuchehaias* show the vizier this proof, he orders each of the ruler's representatives to receive a caftan, and he, like the *tefterdar*, writes a flattering letter to the ruler, that sounds like this: the title is followed by the following:

Üzerinize edası vacib olan cizyenizün malı bu sene-i mübarekede memur olan hazine ağasınun marifeti ile Bâb-ı Âlide mülâzimetde olan kapukethudalarınız bittemam ve lâ-kusur eda ve teslim eylemişlerdür. Aferin! Berhodar olasın!

Şevketlü padişah effendimüz haziretlerinün ekmegi sena helâl olsun! Göreyim seni! Bundan böyle dahi sair hidmet-i padişahîde etek dermeyan idüp var kudretini sarf eyleyesin; hilâfından ihtiraz idüp sadakat u istikametde sabit-i kadem olasun ve selâm!

This means: "The sums of money you owe yearly, were given and sent in full without deceit in this joyful year, through the Great Treasurer sent by us and through your *capuchehaias* that always stay at the Grand Porte for your service. Good job! May you have growth in everything, and may the bread from our Holy Emperor be sustaining. I will see you. Spend the same in the future in service of our Emperor with all the power you have, roll your sleeves and beware of working with hostility, or in another way than the way you were commanded, walk on an honorable and loyal path, and may you have peace, Given...etc.".

Aside from the yearly tribute that I was talking about, at the *bairam* or Turkish Easter, Moldavia must pay a *peșcheș* to the Emperor of twelve thousand five hundred imperials and two furs: one of sable valued at one thousand five hundred imperials, and another of lynx; to the Sultan's *validé*, meaning the Sultan's mother, they must pay five thousand imperials and a lynx fur; six thousand for wax for the Emperor's candles; for tallow used for the Emperor's ships they must pay twelve thousand imperials; for the cîzlar-agasî, the chief of eunuchs, two thousand five hundred leonines and a sable fur; five thousand imperials and a more valuable sable fur for the vizier; five hundred and a sable fur for the reis-effendi. The other gifts that are shared among the servants of the Emperor and the vizier are fabrics, silks, and cheaper sable furs, which they name *paceà*, because they're made from the sable's legs and are rarely worth less than forty thousand imperials.

On top of all this, if a war starts with the Poles or with the Russians, the vizier orders a bridge over the Danube or to have horses gathered for the royal stables, either for pulling the heavy war artillery, or to transport provisions, all this must be done by the country with the greatest of cares, but it lowers the overall yearly tribute. If another ruler must be appointed, he might not have to pay the same tribute, because the candidate's ambition is the one that sets the vizier's limit of greed. The rule, however, asks for the Emperor to be given twenty-five thousand imperials, five thousand to his mother, fifteen thousand for the vizier, half of that for the *chehaia*, a thousand for the *tefterdar,* and five hundred for the *reis-effendi*. The gifts given to the other servants and courtiers go up to forty thousand imperials, just like the *peșcheș* paid at the bairam.

The *ischiemne-agasî*, the one that takes the ruler to his throne, is paid ten thousand leonines. Very often, however, that spending can reach three hundred thousand leonines, not the ruler being the one to pay, but the country. His reign confirmation has its own spending as well. It can be one of two types, big or small. The small one, when he's only given a *hiucm-firmane* or a reign warrant, is bought with twenty-five thousand imperials or fewer, depending on if the vizier feels generous. The big one, when his reign firman gets renewed every three years, requires the same amount of money as when he took the reign. Aside from this, if the *capugi-bașa* or another one of the Emperor's servants is sent to the ruler with a command, they must not leave without gifts.

Chapter XV
About the Moldavian Nobility

Having to research the origins of Moldavia's nobility we can't refer to uncertain and dark traditions as is done by other nations: Greek and Latin writers, cherished by all the scholars of this earth, give us a clearer light than the sun at noon on this matter. I don't think some people believe that Trajan after he defeated Decebal and destroyed his whole kingdom, brought new settlers to Dacia that were not Roman soldiers. If we didn't have the testimony that says that even though Hadrian, after Trajan's death, left other Asian provinces to the barbarians, was however prevented from abandoning Moldavia, only because he was afraid of losing so many thousands of Roman citizens that were settled there. To the reader knowledgeable in Antiquity, it would be enough to remember, to be convinced of this, the long-lasting Roman tradition that prevented them from recruiting men for their legions that were not Roman citizens and especially from a good ancestry. Because of all these facts, I consider it's not worth opposing Aeneas Sylvius' tale, through which he claims that Moldavia was a land where Roman exiles were sent because the testimony of a historian contemporary with the events should never be combated, in order to prefer another's opinion, who a thousand years later can jabber about whatever he can imagine.

I don't plan on talking more about how these things unfolded,[43] because, for so many centuries that passed from Trajan to our days, the Roman nation grew and remained in Dacia; to whoever doubts this we only bring one proof: the language spoken in Moldavia, which resembles the Roman language more than any other, and shows who the founders of our nation are too clearly to claim otherwise.

However, far from us is the idea that the families formerly distinguished among the Romans living in Dacia compared through their ranks to the others are the same as the boyar families that flourish in Moldavia today. The fickleness of human nature is well known to me and I know well that Dragoş, the founder of Moldavia, granted high honor ranks, not to those who had more titles from their ancestors, but to those who surpassed others through bravery and loyalty, and to them he gave political and military jobs. We also know that on Moldavia's fields, ravaged by Tartar invasions, they set up new colonies of peasants brought from Poland and that they gave those newly founded villages their names, or that, more probably, they took the name of the villages as a sign of their nobility. Over time, after the reigns of Serbians and Bulgarians were scattered by Turkish occupation and the seat city of Greece fell under foreign subjugation, is well known that many born in the noblest families of these nations took refuge in Moldavia, which was a place of safety for everyone during those times, and through their loyalty, they were granted land rights and the honor of becoming boyars.

In the same manner, Tartars from good families, either by falling captive during the almost constant wars between the Scythians and

---

[43] *Author's Note:* Because I want to show it in the *Romano-Moldavian Chronicle*.

Moldavians or by surrendering willingly to the ruler because of internal discords, were baptized and were admitted into political and military positions in the country. Then recently, especially during the past century, when Moldavian rulers started to be sent from Constantinople, more slaves, Circassians, and Abkhazians, who were bought from Constantinople where they were working as slaves, after they proved their loyalty to their masters through long services, were lifted in rank, first to court duties, then to boyar titles, and through this, they entered the nobility. The rulers even called some Poles to the ranks of boyars, especially the ones that were on their side in that country, the same way that some Moldavians joined the Polish nobility. Thus, the number of Moldavian boyars grew too much and the rulers decided to divide them into three classes. The first class was obviously given to the ones that received their titles from the ruler himself or the ones of their blood. They are the equivalent of the *boiarski rod* from the Russian Empire, who are also distinguished from the other boyars in this manner.

The second class is held by the courtiers, or people of the court, who inherited one or two villages from their ancestors, which the Russians call *dvoriane*. In the third class are the *călărași* (riders), who in exchange for land given to them by the rulers, are charged with always joining war expeditions at their own expense. The last ones are called *răzeși*, which we rather prefer to call free peasants rather than boyars; they closely resemble the Russian *odnodvorci*, who do not own farmlands, but live in groups in a single village and work the lands either by themselves or use hired servants for it.

The boyar families, the way they're mentioned from the beginning in the history of Moldavia, all exist today and through a miracle of fate, no old family of Moldavian boyars was lost so far, despite all the wars and Tartar invasions, aside from the line of Vasile Lupu, the ruler of Moldavia who, even despite being the highest standing family, today is completely extinct. Even though some of these families ended up being so poor, that from the five thousand households they used to have, they now barely have five, their line remains intact. I believe I should insert the names of these families in alphabetical order because they deserve the same respect:

Abazeștii,

Arbureștii,

Asanii, who according to Choniates originate from Asan, John's brother, the ruler of Wallachia,

Arăpeștii,

Bontășeștii,

Bașoteștii,

Bogdăneștii,

Buhușeștii,

Bălșeștii, two families,

Bouleștii,

Bujorenii,

Burgheleștii,

Cantacuzinii, Greeks originating from John Cantacuzenus, the Emperor of Constantinople,

Cantemirii, originating from the Tauric Chersonese,

Cărăbățeștii,

Carpeștii,

Catargieștii,

Chrisoverghii, Greek, line of rulers,

Clucereștii,

Costacheștii, or Gavrilițeștii,

Costineștii, Serbians,

Cruplenscheștii, Polish

Ciobăneștii,

Ceaureștii,

Cerchizeștii, Circassians,

Țifeștii,

Ciogoleștii,

Darieștii,

Doniceștii,

Draguțeștii,

Duraceștii, or Doneștii,

Frătițeștii,

Găneștii,

Goianeștii,

Hăbășeștii,

Hînceștii,

Hisăreștii,

Isăceștii,

Kiriaceștii,

Mihuleștii,

Micleștii,

Mileștii,

Mereștii,

Movileștii, family counting five rulers,

Moțoceștii,

Murguleștii,

Năculeștii,

Neculeștii, Greek,

Paladieștii, Greek,

Petralifii, Greek,

Pilateștii,

Pisoscheștii, Polish,

Prajeștii,

Racovițeștii,

Razii, Greek,

Ropceneștii,

Ruseteștii, Greek,

Sepoteneștii,

Stîrceștii,

Sturzeștii,

Șeptiliceștii,

Șoldaneștii,

Tălăbeștii,

Tălpeștii,

Tămășeștii,

Tanschii,

Tăutuleștii,

Totoeștii,

Tudoreștii, Greek,

Turculeștii,

Vîrlăneștii,

Urecheștii,

Joreștii,

Zorileștii.

In the old times, there used to be a Moldavian custom that became almost a law through a long tradition, after which the youth, even the ones born in noble families, couldn't get a job with the public service unless they proved themselves loyal through small jobs, and accumulated practice and experience. Because of this, lower-ranked boyars used to give their sons to high-ranked boyars when they came of age, but they couldn't be charged with anything other than to serve the table and guard their master's chamber. After they learned the workings of the court for three years and learned manners, the same boyar presented them to the ruler, and with his help, they obtained a place among the *cămărași* serving the Grand Divan, from where, after a year, they were moved to the small divan and finally to the throne room. There, if any of them showed signs of truly beautiful nature and noble character so that he could be entrusted with important tasks, he was received among the servants of the great hall. After a few years, if any other boyar got involved, because the parents believed it disrespectful to recommend their own son, he was given the role of *postelnicel*, meaning a low-ranked *postelnic*, one of the ones that usually carry in front of the ruler twelve thin white sticks, as tall as them. If through this position he proved his loyalty and skill to the ruler, he was accepted to other secret jobs in the court. After spending his youth this way, he was promoted first to the third rank of nobility, finally, even in the first one. However, if the ruler noticed someone was gifted with a witty mind, he could raise a boyar in a few years from the lowest rank to the highest. Today, however, because people's vanity is growing together with their poverty, a boyar considers his nobility stained if he served a high-rank boyar, but because his ambition doesn't let him live away from the court, he forces himself in every way to be received through his relative's influence, among the closest servants, called *boiernași*, meaning small boyars. Because this class is a sort of nursery of the entire state, from which people of important functions are chosen, it is hard to say what kind of human monsters are elevated many times to the highest positions. And this is the reason why among the boyars above you'll see very often arrogant, flaunty and proud people, that not only are oblivious to how to run a country, but they don't know its traditions and to whom you won't find any reason of praise, aside from one or two of them that might have one good quality from birth, unpolished from the outside and completely uncultivated.

Reaching this point, it might not be unfit to show in which way and with what solemnities the boyars are set in their functions by the ruler of Moldavia. On the last day of the month of December, the eve of Saint Vasile's feast, after the vespers service, all the boyars commanded by the *Great Postelnic*, leave the tokens of their rank in the throne room. The next day, on the first of January, three or four hours before sunrise, all boyars gather at court, the ones in function as well as the ones removed, and follow their ruler to church to take part in the morning service. After it ends, the ruler enters the throne room and sits on his throne and the boyars stop in the small divan. Then the ruler commands his closest cămăraș to summon the *Great Postelnic* if he wants to be strengthened in his function, if not, the one decided to be his successor. As soon as he arrives, the ruler tells him a few words, and reminds him of the services done for the country by either his parents or himself, adding that this is the reason for strengthening his position or for obtaining it, he advises him to keep being loyal, letting him know of the rewards he'd get, also of the punishments, and teaches him what his duties consist of. After telling him all these he hands him the silver staff, which he receives after kissing the ruler's hand and his robe, and he's then dressed in a caftan by the *Great Cămăraș*. Also, the *Great Postelnic* is the first to receive the symbols of his power, not because he is above all the others, because as I said before he's the fifth in rank, but because all the others must be introduced by him.

Therefore, because he was the first one, at the ruler's command he summons the one the ruler wants to grant the *logofăt* position to; he addresses him in a short speech, gives him the gold staff and the *Great Postelnic* sets the *caftan* on his shoulders, and gently supporting him from his underarms takes him to kiss the ruler's hand and robe. The same service is done to the other advisers and boyars of the first rank. The second-rank boyars are called by the second postelnic and dressed in caftan; the third-rank boyars are called by the third postelnic, but they're not given a caftan, only strengthened in their positions at the ruler's command.

After this ceremony they all accompany the ruler who goes to the holy service; in the church, the ones new in function take the seats of the ones who were removed, and the ones who were removed, together with other of their colleagues remain in the church narthex. After the service ends the ruler calls whoever wants to join him for his meal, and in the evening, he sends each adviser and first-rank boyar two silver goblets with a capacity of around two pounds each, and each second-rank boyar a goblet from which they all drink wine in front of the ruler.

The wives of the first-rank boyars are gifted on the same day by the ruler's wife with a small goblet each. The next day the boyars gather again in the receiving hall, thank the ruler for his generosity and each offers him a gift through the postelnic, either a horse or something else of value.

The boyars' wives bring the same honors to the ruler's wife on the same day, inside the women's chamber.

For the rest of the year the ruler rarely changes anything in the public functions, even though nothing prevents him from replacing them whenever he wants. But because the custom dictates for positions to be given or changed at the beginning of the year, the rulers, probably urged by respect for long traditions, decided to keep the dates their ancestors considered right for these ceremonies.

Chapter XVI
About the Other Inhabitants of Moldavia

It is hard to believe that another closed country exists with borders as tight as Moldavia, which can encompass so many nations. Aside from the Moldavians, whose ancestors came from Maramureș, Moldavia is inhabited by many Greeks, Serbians, Bulgarians, Poles, Kazakhs, Russians, Hungarians, Germans, Armenians, Jews, and a fast-growing community of Gypsies. The Greeks, Albanians, Serbians, and Bulgarians live here freely, and some work in trade, while others serve the ruler in the military for a good salary. The Germans, Polish, and Kazakhs are few, and they're either soldiers or court servants; some Poles even became boyars, but that happens rarely.

The Armenians are considered subjects, just like the townsfolk and merchants from other cities and markets of Moldavia, and pay the same taxes as them; however, just like the Romano-Catholic Christians, they have their own churches, as great and beautiful as the Orthodox churches, and enjoy the freedom of religion.

The Jews are also considered subjects, and they're indebted to pay a special yearly fee, bigger than the usual one; they don't engage in any trade aside from being merchants and innkeepers, and they can have synagogues wherever they want but made out of wood, not stone. The Russians and the Hungarians have always been serfs in Moldavia.

Gypsies are spread all over the country; there's almost no boyar that doesn't have multiple Gypsy families in his care. From where these people came to Moldavia I don't even know, nor say our chronicles. All Gypsies speak the same language in these lands, mixed with many pure Greek words, even with Persian words. They don't have other trades aside from ironwork and working with gold. They have the same nature and the same bad habits all over the country; their supreme virtue and main characteristics are theft and laziness.

There are many Turks in Iași and in other cities that deal with trading, but they're not allowed to buy land anywhere or build a house in any village or city, especially not a church, but the Ottoman Porte never insisted for the rulers to allow this. It would be better if they never spoke either!

True Moldavians, aside from the boyars whose classes I showed you above, are either townsfolk or peasants. The townsfolk are the ones living in cities and markets, and the peasants are the ones living in villages. The ones living in cities are not anyone's subjects but the ruler's, and they only pay taxes to him. All of them are craftsmen; a Moldavian is rarely a merchant. Because Moldavians are very vain and lazy from birth, they consider being a merchant shameful, aside from selling produce from their own lands. I believe this is the reason why rich merchants are rare in Moldavia, even though our country exports more goods to foreign lands than it receives from them, and somehow it always suffers from a lack of money. The foreign merchants: Turks, Jews, Armenians, and Greeks, who we usually call *gelepi*, ended up owning all of Moldavia's commerce because of our indifference, taking to Constantinople and to other cities whole herds of sheep and cattle bought for a small price from Moldavia, that they sell for two or three times the price in other lands.

However, because a big part of them can't own lands and houses in Moldavia, most of their money is spent outside the country, a small part of it returning from beyond the Danube, becoming part of the tribute owed to the Turks or being used for other communal needs.

Pure Moldavian peasants don't exist, and they either originate from Russia or Transylvania, which we usually call *ungureni*. In the first century after Moldavia was founded, because Dragoș found the new country void of inhabitants, he shared it with the ones that accompanied him on his expedition. But because it seemed unfair for a noble to work for another noble, because all those who were born from Roman seed were considered nobles, and because a nation used to handle weapons believed it was below them to work the fields, Dragoș' companions were constrained, with their ruler's blessing, to pray on neighboring lands where peasant serfdom was used, to take these peasants and move them on their lands. This is proven by the Moldavian word for peasant, which is *vecin* (neighbor), and shows that those who were forced by Moldavian weapons to work on their lands were previously their neighbors. For this reason, in upper Moldavia, which was first inhabited by the Drăgoșesti, there are many peasant households, but in lower Moldavia, land that was inhabited later, there are only the peasants that boyars bought from upper Moldavia or *răzeși* who sold their properties because of poverty, and who were forced by the boyars to obey them. That's why during trials if a boyar claims that any peasant is his serf, it's easy to see whose estate he belongs to. If the accused can show that his predecessors owned a piece of land, even if it was lost because of poverty or the hostility of those times, or that they were received among the riders, courtiers, or pages, he is declared completely free, because only a free man can be charged with these duties; if he can't prove any of it, it is implied that he is a boyar's serf. The ones who were brought to Moldavia from Poland and forgot their native tongue with time adopted the Moldavian language; however, the ones that live on the border with Poland speak Ruthenian and Polish dialects. Hungarians were the most tenacious ones, keeping their native tongue and their Catholic religion, but all of them can speak Moldavian. However, whatever type of peasants they are, they all have to work the fields for their masters; it's their master's decision how many days a week they make them work. The boyar cannot take away their money or livestock, and if any peasant found a hidden treasure, their master can't ask for any part of it; if he took it, he would be sent to court for trial and forced to give it back. If, however, the master wanted to cause a peasant any injustice, he could beat him until he willingly gave him whatever he wanted.

It's forbidden by law for any boyar to kill a servant, and if he caused his death in any way, the master would be found guilty of murder and forced to free the wife and children of the victim. Nobody has the right of life or death over any Moldavian, because this is a right only the ruler has. A high boyar in Moldavia can also sell his subjects, but not outside the village where that subject was born; if, however, he sells the whole estate together with the peasants living there, that transaction is considered legal. The peasant must pay taxes according to the ruler's will and these taxes are not of a fixed amount and don't have a certain limit.

About the Other Inhabitants of Moldavia

In a word, I'd say that among all field workers, as many as there are in the world, the most oppressed ones are the Moldavian peasants, if their crops couldn't somehow take them out of their poverty without their will.

They're very lazy, work only if they're forced to, plow rarely, sow little, but harvest a lot. They don't care about having as much as they can through their work; they're satisfied with gathering enough in their granary for a year, or as they usually call it, until it's time for new bread. That's why if they have a bad year or if an enemy attack prevents the harvest, they're prone to starve. If the peasant has one or two cows, he thinks he has enough to feed his whole family. Some cows give forty liters of milk daily, or at least twenty-four. And if the peasant has twenty beehives, he can easily pay his yearly taxes with what he earns from them. Leaving aside the fact that a single beehive, if the weather allows, creates seven others in a year, each of them gives two or more measures of honey, and one measure is worth an imperial.

The ones living in the mountains have plenty of sheep, honey, and fruits; the ones from the lowlands have grains, bulls, and horses. Their worst misfortune is that their neighbors are the Tartars, who not only steal whatever they can but sometimes start wars with Poland and have to pass through Moldavia, causing a lot of damage and sometimes taking villagers as slaves and selling them in Constantinople, claiming that they're Russians. These invasions were indeed stopped recently on the Sultan's command, repeated multiple times. But who can defend themselves from the Tartar's deception? The ones taken to Constantinople by fate are luckier. There the ruler's *capuchehaias* can take a Moldavian slave without pay, wherever they found him, and free him.

Everything I said above about Moldavia's peasants must not be applied to all three lands of Moldavia, where even if they're not nobles, are under no boyar's command, and they form a sort of republic. The first one is Câmpulung, in the land of Suceava, surrounded by a very long row of tall mountains. It contains around fifteen villages, which have their own laws. Sometimes they receive two *vornici* sent by the ruler, and not rarely, if they offend the peasants they are banished, using the defense methods nature gave them.

They don't know how to work the fields, which they don't even have in the mountains, and their whole work is related to sheep. They pay an annual tribute, not as much as the ruler asks for, but as much as they promise the ruler, and this agreement is renewed through their envoys every time a new ruler is chosen. If the ruler wants to be more severe and cause them hardships, they don't argue for long, refuse to pay the tribute completely, and retreat into the mountains; this is the reason why the rulers don't ask for more than they're offered. Incited a few times by rebels, they refused to deal with the ruler and received protection from the Poles; this made some historians claim that Moldavia paid tribute to Poland. However, everyone knows, and this fact is supported by the testimony of the bishop of Premisl Piasecius, whatever would say Długosz, Sarnicius, and Orichovius, that Moldavia, before being subjugated by Turks, was Poland's ally; and after it started paying tribute to the Turks, the Poles didn't even think about bringing Moldavia under their control, some of their kings rather tried to reclaim their old freedom.

The second republic in Moldavia, which is small, is Vrancea, in the lands of Putna, close to the border with Wallachia, surrounded everywhere by wild mountains. It has twelve villages, two thousand households, and, just as Câmpulung, deals with shepherding, not knowing anything about fieldwork. The people there also pay the ruler a tribute that they decide, have their own laws, and don't receive commands or judges from the ruler.

The third one is Tigheci in the land of Fălciul, which is a forest bordering the Tartars from Bugeac, and it's the strongest wall of Moldavia between the Prut River and Bessarabia. Its inhabitants pay a small tribute to the ruler and all of them are *călăraşi* (riders). In times past, they used to be eight thousand, today there are hardly two thousand left; however, they surpass all Moldavians in bravery. It's said in an old proverb "Five Tartars from Crimea are worth more than ten Tartars from Buceag, five Moldavians are worth more than ten Tartars from Crimea, but five *condreni* (because this is the name used for the riders in Tigheci) beat ten Moldavians." I spoke more about them in the first part of the book, the sixth chapter.

Chapter XVII
About the Customs of Moldavia

Having to describe Moldavians' habits, a subject that was unknown to foreigners before, my love for my country urges and commands me to praise the nation in which I was born, and put its inhabitants in a good light; contrariwise my love for truth prevents me from praising things that my judgment urges me to criticize. I think a country should put out in the open, under the people's eyes, the multitude of sins they have, instead of allowing them to cheat through bitter flattery and clever exoneration, so that they would believe that everything they do is right, while everyone else that has better manners criticizes this behavior.

Defeated by the arguments of this love for truth, I sincerely confess that aside from the Orthodox faith and hospitality, we could scarcely find something to praise among the Moldavians' habits. All the vices found in other people, rule over the Moldavians as well, if not always in a great measure, surely not in a small one; their qualities, however, are rare, because they lack good education and the exercise of their virtues. You'll hardly find a person that shines among others through virtue unless he was helped by a gift from birth. Pride is their mother and vanity is their sister; if a Moldavian owns a fancy horse and weapons to brag about, he thinks nobody surpasses him; he doesn't shy away from fighting with God if need be. Generally, they're bold and ready to fight, however, they calm down fast and reconcile with their adversary. The word "duel" is not known to them. The peasants rarely go from words to weapons; they shut their loud neighbors up with clubs, whips, and fists; the same goes for soldiers, who hardly go from fist fighting to weapons, and if it sometimes happens, they get punished severely.

Moldavians are funny and joyful, and their heart is not far from their mouth, but even if they forget grudges fast, they also forget about friendships. They don't shy away from drunkenness, but don't look for it either; their greatest joy is to eat from the sixth hour of the day till the third hour of the night, sometimes until sunrise, and to stuff themselves with wine until they throw up. However, they don't do this every day, only during feast days or during bad winter weather, when the cold locks them in their houses and urges them to warm their limbs with wine. Only soldiers like brandy; the others only drink one small cup before noon. They mostly love wine, especially the one from lower Moldavia or the one made along the border with Wallachia.

There was once a contest between Wallachians and Moldavians to choose the finest drinkers; the champions were taken to the bridge at Focșani, which is the border between Moldavia and Wallachia. They fought fiercely by emptying glasses, until the one from Wallachia died, losing his breath from all the wine he drank; as a reward for his victory, the Moldavian was made a boyar by the ruler. They can shoot with a bow and arrow, and they can even throw spears, but their greatest talent is with the sword. Guns are only used by hunters because they don't consider it honorable to use a weapon that requires no skill against the enemy. For their first attack, they always appear very fierce, softer for the second one, but if they're deflected again, they rarely dare to attack again. However, they learned from Tartars to turn around while running, and with this trick, they took the victory away from their enemy multiple times. With the ones they defeat, they are either gentle or cruel, depending on their fickle nature. To kill a Turk or a Tartar is considered to be a Christian duty and the one that treated them kindly they consider that he strayed from his faith. The way of judging such matters was shown during the last invasion of Bugeac when Petriceico, following the disaster at Vienna, attacked Bessarabia.

They don't have any limit: when they are doing well, they become arrogant; when they're doing badly, they become discouraged. At first glance, they don't think anything is difficult; if they encounter even the smallest obstacle, they become troubled and don't know what to do. If they see their attempts are in vain, they repent too late for what they did. Thus, it is only possible to attribute it to the unspoken will of the divine that the uneducated and weak Moldavian nation could not be subjugated by the mighty and fearsome Ottoman Empire, which had overthrown the Roman occupation of Asia and much of Europe, conquered Hungary, Serbia, Bulgaria, and numerous other kingdoms, and forcibly subdued the intelligent Greek nation. Despite the Ottoman's attempts to shake off the willing submission of Moldavia and their repeated efforts to force them into submission by the sword, they refrained from tampering with their political and religious laws.

Again, not only do the Moldavians not like education, they almost hate it. Not even the names of sciences and arts are known to them. They believe that scholars are not in their right minds, so much so that if they want to praise someone's knowledge, they say he ended up crazy because of too much learning. In this regard, a very foolish saying that can be heard often from Moldavians' mouths, is that knowledge is the business of priests, for the rest is enough to know how to read and write, to sign their names, and to be able to write in registers which bulls are white, black, horned, their horses, sheep, cows, beehives, and others; everything else is useless.

Even though women are not forbidden to show themselves to men as harshly as Turks demand of their women, however, if they're from a good family they rarely wander away from their home without a reason. Noblewomen are indeed beautiful but not as beautiful as simple ones; all peasants surpass them in beauty, but they're frivolous and full of disgraceful habits. Some drink heavily when inside their homes, but it's rare to see a drunk woman in public. The less a woman drinks and eats as a guest, the more honorable she is considered. That's why you will rarely see a woman take a bite of bread, and she'll part her lips to show her teeth while trying to hide when she takes the bite. They don't consider anything more shameful than a married or widowed woman with her hair showing and a woman with her head bare in public is considered shameful. Contrary to that, girls find it shameful to wear any type of kerchief, because an uncovered head is a sign of maidenhood. In the same way, the climate is different across Moldavia, the same are the habits.

People of lower Moldavia, fouled by so many wars with the Tartars, are better and fiercer, but at the same time restless and fickle: if they don't have a foreign enemy to fight, they often turn because of their laziness and rebel against their captains, and not rarely against their ruler.

Few people care about religion. Most of them, including most of the lower class, believe that every person's fate was decided by God, including the day they'll die and nobody can die in a war if their time didn't come; this gives them such courage that sometimes they savagely attack their enemies, convinced of the fact that killing or praying on a Turk, a Scythe, or a Jew is not a sin or a crime. The ones living close to Tartars steal and pray on them, and if they invaded Tartar lands, they say they didn't take their belongings but instead took theirs back because the Tartars nowadays wouldn't own anything if they wouldn't have taken everything from the Moldavians' ancestors.

Adultery is rare, and young people don't find it shameful, but a reason to brag, because until they get married, making love in hiding is like they were free from any law; that's why you can often hear from them the saying: "my son, beware of theft or robbery because I won't be able to save you from hanging; but no death sentence awaits you for forbidden togetherness, as long as you'll pay money for *şugubinat*" (that's how they call the one looking for unfaithful girls and depraved women).

However, we always have to praise the hospitality they show to strangers and travelers. It's true that even though they're poor because of the Tartars, they never refuse bread and boarding to visitors, feeding them and their horses for three days at no cost. They receive travelers with open hearts and joyful expressions like they receive a brother or a relative. Some even delay their lunch until the ninth hour of the day and, to avoid eating alone, they ask servants to wait in the road and to bring back whatever passer-by they met. Only the townsfolk of Vaslui are not known for this, because not only do they close their homes and pantries to visitors, but if they see they have a guest they stealthily retreat just to return dressed in tattered clothing and pretend to be beggars to travelers.

The inhabitants of upper Moldavia are not warriors, and they don't desire fights, they just prefer earning their bread through hard work. They're more religious and prone to superstitions, that's why in the lands of Suceava there are sixty stone churches and over two hundred stone monasteries in all upper Moldavia. The mountains are full of monks and hermits that dedicate their lonely lives to God, far from the world's troubles.

Thefts are few among them or not present at all, they've always shown their loyalty to the ruler, and even though they had internal struggles they didn't start rebellions, aside from the boyars in lower Moldavia. They keep boldly purity and beautiful habits even before marriage, which is rare to see among Moldavians from the lower country. They are more skilled than the rest when it comes to conducting communal affairs, and they take better care of their fortunes, eagerly obey commands given to them, and pay more mind to visitors than the ones from lower Moldavia.

Moldavian dancing is different from other nations. They don't dance in pairs or in groups of four, like the French or the Poles, but groups of more people form either a circle or a long row, a thing only done easily at weddings. When dancing they all clasp hands in a circle and move at an equally measured pace from right to left, a dance called the *hora*; when dancing in a row, they also clasp their hands, but to keep the ends of the row open they turn with different directions, naming this dance *danț*, which is a Polish word. At weddings, before the priest's blessing unites the lovers, the custom is for people to dance in yards and on the roads in two rows, one row for women and one for men. Each row chooses a leader, an old and honorable person, who holds a golden staff covered in flowers or painted in multiple colors, with an embroidered kerchief on its end. For the first step, one of the leaders pulls the row behind him from right to left and the other pulls them from left to right, so the dancers face each other, after which they turn back-to-back; then each row turns in curving moves, but slowly enough to not blend, so you could hardly tell they're moving. In both rows each has their place according to their rank: boyars' women and girls enjoy the same honors as the men and their parents. The first place is always taken by the leader of the dance, the second place is held by the godfather, and the third by the groom. The godmother and the bride have the same places in the women's row, even if they're way lower in rank than the rest. After the wedding, both rows blend and spin in a circle in a way that each married man holds their wife by the hand, and each unmarried man holds a girl of the same rank, spinning. Sometimes they dance the *hora* with three corners, four corners, egg-shaped, or in other irregular shapes, depending on the leader's wish.

Aside from all these types of festive dances, they have another magical one, which requires an uneven number of dancers: seven, nine, or eleven. These are called *călușari*, and they gather once a year dressed in women's clothing, wear braided crowns on their heads made of wormwood leaves and flowers, change their voices to sound like women, and to not be recognized cover their faces with a white cloth.

They carry bared swords in their hands, which they would use to stab any man who'd dare to rip off their face covers. This right was given to them by an old custom in a way that they couldn't even be charged for killing a man. The leader of the group is called *starețʉ*, the second dancer is called *primicer* and his role is to ask the *starețʉ* what dance he wants to execute, and then he tells it to the other dancers secretly, so the crown couldn't hear the name before seeing it.

They know over a hundred rhythms and dances, some so beautiful that it seems they don't touch the ground while dancing but float in the air. For ten days, between the Ascension and Whitsuntide holidays, they don't rest but travel the cities and villages dancing and running. During this time, they only sleep in churches, convinced that if they sleep anywhere else they'd be caught by fairies, which they call *frumoasele*. If a group of *calușari* meets another group on the way, they must fight, and the losers make way after discussing the terms of peace, and losers agree to admit they're beneath the other group for nine years. If in a fight someone gets killed, it is not brought to trial and it is not even searched for who the killer was. Once received in a group, a person must travel with it every year for nine years; and if he leaves, they say he's haunted by evil spirits and tormented by fairies. The superstitious crowd believes they have the power to banish chronic illnesses and the healing is done in the following way: after the sufferer lies on the ground, they start dancing and, at a specific point during their song, they each step on him from his head to his toes, finally they whisper something in his ear and command the sickness to leave his body. After doing this for three days, it often results in hope and difficult sicknesses that multiple healers and doctors attempted to cure, disappear without a trace in this way: this is how strong the power of faith is, even when it comes to superstitions.

Chapter XVIII
About Engagements and Weddings in Moldavia

After I talked about the nature and customs in Moldavia, the reader would not be displeased if I talked a bit about the Moldavian traditions when it comes to engagements and weddings. Moldavians have their children married when they reach an age that allows the holy canons of marriage. However, it's considered disgraceful for a girl to look for a husband and the country's customs require the young man to be the one looking for a wife, not for the girl's parents to look for a son-in-law either. Therefore, if a young man likes a girl, he sends *pețitori* (suitors), a word originating from the Latin *petitores*. The suitors try to guess the parents' thoughts, so they don't embarrass themselves in front of anyone if they get rejected by any chance, and if they accept the offer, the young man's relatives gather and go to the girl's house. Then the leader of the suitors, named *staroste*, works on a short speech, which is spoken the same almost everywhere, so I don't think it's a bad thing for me to write it down here: "Our ancestors, grandparents, and great-grandparents, hunting through forests found the land on which we live today, that feeds us and feasts us with its milk and honey. Drawn by their example, our glorious master such and such named, hunting through plains, forests, and mountains, met a shy and obedient deer, that didn't even allow him to watch it, but ran and hid in its lair. Following its tracks, we reached this house; that's why you must surrender our prey, which we found through our labors, or show us which way it went." At this, the speaker adds whatever other metaphors he comes up with within his mind. At first, the parents tell him no such prey came to their house, and they probably went the wrong way, and the deer might be hiding among their neighbors. When the suitors keep insisting, they are brought an old, ugly servant dressed in rags, and they are asked if that's the deer they're looking for. The suitors deny it and claim their prey has golden hair, falcon eyes, beaded teeth, lips redder than cherries, a lionțs waist, goose chest, swan neck, fingers smoother than wax, and a face brighter than the sun and the moon. When the parents claim again, they've never seen it, the suitors reply they have good hounds that are never wrong, and they told them the deer is hiding there. Finally, when the suitors threaten with the use of force and weapons, the parents bring forth the girl, adorned as much as their status permits and the suitors tell them that's the deer they were looking for. Then they call for the priest, and if he's busy with other duties, they call for older people close by, in front of which the lovers exchange rings. After this ceremony, the parents immediately hide the girl from prying eyes, and they lay a family feast where they don't leave until the wedding date is decided.

But when the boyars' children get married, no engagement or religious ceremony can be done without the ruler's approval and without proof from the bishop. Proof is needed to prevent marriages among people stopped by divine and religious laws, and the ruler's approval, to prevent marriage between closely related boyar families.

And after the wedding date is set, the month before it, after the religious service, relatives of the groom and bride, gather at both of their homes, bringing with them local musicians that are almost always Gypsies, and while they sing their usual songs and play their instruments, they have a small party in the house.

In the afternoon, the servants and other ladies of the house sift the flour meant for the wedding feast, which is why this day is called "sifting day."

If the lovers' homes are in the same town or village, or if they're not more than three days away from each other, the wedding feasts start at both homes the following Thursday and last until Saturday. On Sunday, all blood relatives and the other kinsfolk of the groom gather to bring the bride and send *colăcari* (wedding riders) ahead to announce the groom's coming. The bride's guests set traps for them on the road and try to catch them before they reach her house, and the riders use the fastest horses they can find to avoid being caught. Nevertheless, if they get caught, if they're lower class they get tied up, put back on their horses, and sent back, but if they're upper class, they're surrounded by the bride's relatives and taken to her house under guard. When they get there, they're asked what their business is, and they reply that they were sent to declare war and an army will arrive shortly to occupy the fortress. After these words, the announcer is taken to the house and forced to drink a few big cups of wine and, when he gets very drunk, he's allowed to leave accompanied by some of the bride's guests. When they see the groom coming, they release the rider throwing mocking jokes at him and run back home, but if the groom's companions can catch them, they tie them up and take them with them.

Finally, when all the guests gather at the bride's home they organize a horse race, and the reward is decided: for the common folk it is a beautifully crafted towel and for the richer ones it is a piece of expensive fabric or silk. After they send men to set the target, the announcer gives the start of the race, and hearing his voice, the ones that think they have better horses start hitting the spurs. The winner receives the prize from the bride, and the horse is adorned with a crown of flowers, beautifully braided.

After Vespers, finally, the lovers are accompanied by a great convoy to the church to be married religiously. In the middle of the church is laid a carpet, where on the right stands the groom and on the left the bride. Meanwhile, under their feet, their families set gold coins or leonines for the lower classes, and though this is meant they have to say goodbye to the world and step on its brilliance. Behind them stand the godparents holding two candles of the same lengths and the same thickness. Meanwhile, the priest recites the prayers for the religious wedding and switches the rings three times.

After putting the wedding crowns on their heads, he walks them through the church like in a dance, while the cantors sing the troparion called "Isaie dances." While this is happening, the family throws coins, nuts, and hop seeds, which are symbols through which they ask God, the giver of life, for fruitfulness, for hops and nuts, and tell him they reject riches and other temptations of the world. Finally, the priest gives them three bites out of a dry slice of bread with honey, a symbol of a permanent union, but to make the guests at the ceremony laugh, he fools them, making them open their mouths three times before letting them bite out of it.

After the end of this ceremony, they all return to the bride's house in the same order in which they came, covering the bride's face with a thin red veil of silk, held in place by two arrows. These are shot in the wall with a bow when the brothers or relatives of the bride take the lovers in their sleeping chamber.

Meanwhile, everyone feasts and drinks until the third hour of the night; after that, the cooks set on the table a grilled rooster with feathers, and one of the guests hides under the table imitating the rooster's song to announce the sunrise. After giving the cooks a tip, they all stand up, and the groom sits in the middle of the room holding his bride by the right hand. Then a scribe reads aloud the dowry document with all the items that were previously set in a room for everyone to see, after which they're loaded on carts to be taken to the groom's house. After the reading, an intermediary of the bride addresses her parents in her name, talks of her birth, upbringing, and all the goods she received from them, thanks them for everything and asks for their blessing. The parents, either themselves or through someone else, give them their blessing, pray to God and to the guardian angel to give them love in marriage and peace and, finally, toasting for their health, which is called *pahar de cale albă* (glass for the white road), accompany them out of the house.

When they're about to go out the door, the brothers or uncles of the bride stop them in the way with unsheathed swords set across the doorway, not letting them pass. The groom convinces them by giving them a horse or another gift which he prepared in advance, and the bride accompanied by the mother or sister of the groom (because she's not allowed to take any servant from her parents' house) gets in the carriage and follows the groom. When they reach his house, after serving a few more glasses of wine, the newlyweds are taken to their room by their godparents. The groom makes sure the bride's parents don't get any information about their daughter the next day.

On the third day, they must come and see their daughter together with all their relatives, a journey called *cale premare*, because disgrace might come out of it, depending on the circumstances.

If it's found that their daughter was a maiden, everything is right and the parents are received with great honors and feast, and after the second course, they're brought the nightgown that shows their daughter's honor, which is set on a table and shown to everyone who must leave a small gift on it in return. This is only done by lower-class folk; in the high class, only the parents-in-law can see it. If the girl stained her honor by making a mistake with someone else, the next day the groom summons his relatives and tells them he found an unclean bride (because that's what they call the girls that are not maidens). They ready a cart in bad shape with broken reigns, and when her parents come, they harness them to the cart instead of bulls, beat them, and force them to take their disgraced daughter back home. Nobody is allowed on the way to help them, and if anyone attempted to free them, aside from getting beaten they are also punished by a judge as someone who doesn't follow the laws. The groom keeps all the dowry and if he spent anything for the wedding he goes to court and asks for the money back from the parents of the girl for not taking care of her honor.

This mockery is only suffered by peasants because boyars keep their daughters closer, so they would rarely have any chance to be dishonored, but if one of them is found to be unclean, they either repair her chastity by endowing her with more villages or more money, of, if the groom doesn't agree to anything, they take her back home and give him the freedom to find another wife.

When the ruler is a godparent, the wedding feast is done at court. The groom receives a hat made of lamb's wool similar to the ruler's, and a horse, and during the feast, he must sit on his right side with his head always covered. All servants stay by his side like he was the ruler, and when he goes to church or returns home, the whole court retinue, with *darabans* and other musical instruments, Christian and Turkish, follow him like he was the ruler. The third day after that, to show his gratitude for the given honors, he comes with his bride and brings gifts for the ruler and his wife.

Chapter XIX
About Funerals in Moldavia

Moldavians do the funeral ceremonies according to the canons of the Oriental Church. As soon as a person gives their last breath, they are washed with warm water, and before their body goes stiff, they're dressed in new clothes that were prepared in advance, lain in the coffin, and set in the great room of the house; they're not taken to the grave on the first day, but they wait until the third day, to avoid them being buried alive from losing their consciousness and being believed dead. All the neighbors are invited to the funeral by the tolling of the bells, and they all show their grief to the relatives of the deceased. Finally, on the day decided for the funeral, everyone gathers around, and after listening to the religious service, they accompany the deceased to the church, with the priest walking ahead and the relatives behind him, and after the religious ceremonies are finished, they bury them in the churchyard.

If the deceased was an army commander, his horses are covered with black blankets, and he's dressed in the best clothes he owned. A spear on which an unsheathed sword is hung, with the handle pointing to the ground, is carried ahead of the coffin; a few soldiers dressed in mail and wearing helmets walk in tight rows on both sides of the coffin. Onion juice or gunpowder is rubbed on the horse's eyes to make them look like they're crying for their master, the same way that people do.

If a boyar dies, the ruler together with all the court retinue accompanies the coffin, and if he was one of the high boyars, the symbol of his office is carried ahead of the coffin until they reach the grave, then it's placed in the throne room or the divan. His seat and position must be kept unoccupied for at least three days.

Not everyone shows their grief in the same way. A peasant's sons, after his death, must keep their head bare for six months, even during winter, and they must let their hair and beard grow; they can't cover their heads even if they had to go on a long journey. In times past, the high-class folk used to do the same for forty days, however, they now discarded these superstitions, preferring to dress in dark clothes and let their hair grow. The sister of a peasant, when her brother dies, usually cuts a strand of her hair and ties it to his cross, making sure it doesn't fall off or is not stolen for a year; if that happens, she cuts another one. Generally, everyone gathers at the grave every Saturday, for a whole year, to mourn their dead.

Rich women hire wailers know many wails through which they depict unhappiness and the emptiness of human life, which can be seen from the verses in which all wails start:

For the world, I sing with mourning
The terrible life,
The way it breaks and is cut
Like it was a thread.

After the ceremony, the wailers evoke the name of the deceased as if he were present, asking him many questions. They pretend he does not want to answer, disgusted by this world. Eventually, at their urging, they pretend he speaks a few words and instructs them on what they must do and fear. He also tells them he will not speak to them again nor return, as he now knows the heaven that God offers to all Christians.

Part III
Religion and Literature

Chapter I
About the Religion of Moldavia

Because of our ancestors' indifference, we don't know what religion the old inhabitants of Moldavia had before the sun of justice rose in these parts. We, however, believe that Dacians originate from Scythians, an opinion shared by all the historians we know, and we're allowed to suspect through a presumption that is not absurd, that they prayed to the same divine forces that Russian chronicles tell us were venerated by the other Scythian nations: Peruna, the god of thunder, Volos, the god of cattle, Pohvist, the god of air, Lado, the god of joy, Kupalo, god of harvest, and other idols of this kind, Osliado, Horsa, Dajuba, Striba, Semargle, and Mocosa.[44]

After the Romans occupied Dacia, because this nation surpassed all when it came to religious superstitions, not only did they not remove the old cults, but according to their tradition, they brought new deities with them. Every time the Romans conquered a new territory, they brought sacrifices to the gods of the defeated nation, the same

---

[44] In fact, Dacians practiced a monotheistic religion, worshipping the god Zalmoxis as decribed by Herodotus. See Kurt W. Treptow, "A Study in Geto-Dacian Religion: The Cult of Zalmoxis." *East European Quarterly*, XXI:4 (Winter, 1987), pp. 501-515. Reprinted: Kurt W. Treptow. *From Zalmoxis to Jan Palach: Studies in East European History*. New York: East European Monographs, Columbia University Press, 1992.

way they did to their own gods; even more, after Egypt's submission, which was a source of rebellions, they brought many idols from there to Rome, where their cult was adopted.

To this, we must add the faith of all the others who prayed to idols, because not only that every country has its own faith, but every family had their own protecting deities, that take care of it and if not persuaded, nobody can rule the country or live peacefully in that family's home.

But when certain pagan faiths disappeared in Moldavia and when this nation received the law of Christ cannot be proven by any historical testimony, but it's agreed upon the fact that the public cult of the Christian religion was not brought to Dacia until the reign of Constantine the Great. The documents of the synod gathered at Sardica prove that during the time of Constantine, the son of Constantine the Great, both lands of Dacia had their own bishop, even if many probably carried Christ's flag long before, convinced by the bloodstained speeches of martyrs.

Today the county confesses the Christian law and holds to the Eastern Church. In no part of their faith are they inclined towards heresies. They don't set aside anything commanded by this religion and don't do anything that is forbidden to them. There has never been seen a heretic in Moldavia, but the country wasn't able to develop, probably because they didn't want to know anything about school theology and other sophisticated crafts of dialectics, but believed that the simple words of the Bible and the teachings of the priests were enough, even without much school, to purify the soul. There is no other rite they hate more than the Roman one, even though the Hungarians, their subjects, keep close to that cult and have their own bishop in Bacău. They say the other heresies are easily seen and it can be noticed they strayed from the true Church: the Papists (because they don't name them Catholics unless they are sons of the Eastern Church) hide a wolf's nature under a sheep's skin, call "brothers" the ones who follow the Greek Church, other times call them "schismatics" and ἀκέφαλοι (without head), because they don't follow the Pope, who's the head of the Church. Sometimes they even call them heretics, which is why the uneducated population can rarely distinguish the truth from a lie and look out for their poison. And to shortly touch on this matter, the strongest proof against any change seems to be this firmness through which Moldavians hold on to the Eastern Church. Is well-known by everyone educated in the history of religions that Transylvania and Hungary, which was the home of our people before Moldavia was founded, never obeyed Constantinople's throne, but the Roman one and its people, so all the inhabitants of these lands, before Luther's and Calvin's sects entered these regions, were sons of the Occidental Church. But because the companions of Dragoș kept their old religion (because there's no proof they abandoned the Occidental Church to receive the Oriental rites) and because it matches the Oriental one in every aspect, it's clear that the same teaching, which now is kept only in the East, was followed in old times in the West, therefore, the Occident is the one that strayed from Christ's true faith, not the Orient. After this detour, we should, however, follow our course.

The symbol of our faith is spoken during the service in a simple manner, the same that was designed by the holy fathers of the Niceea synod, and rejects the papist phrase "and of the Son." They believe exactly what John the Evangelist says through Christ's words about the procession of the Holy Spirit. And as they don't want to receive the procession "of the Son," adding something not in the holy scriptures, they also do not use during services the phrase introduced by Palamas, "only from the Father." They acknowledge seven holy mysteries and do the liturgy following the example of Saint Basil the Great and Saint John Chrysostom. During this liturgy, they use leavened bread, and they follow the communion in both its forms [with bread and with wine]. They honor the holy icons, not carved, but painted, but their prayers are only addressed to the divine being. They believe that saints didn't yet reach absolute happiness, but they still wait together with Peter for the judgment day, and during this time strong hope and faith in it fill their souls and give them unspoken happiness, so much that they don't lack anything for their worth. Also, they don't acknowledge any type of purgatory but believe that light sins are forgiven even after death by prayers at church and charity. They admit and read the holy scripture at church, in the translation of the seventy, rejecting the Vulgata and other translations.

Aside from the fact they fast every Wednesday and Friday, they also fast four times a year at definite intervals; during the great fasting of forty days and in the first days of August dedicated to the Virgin Mary they also abstain from fish. Some very superstitious people don't eat meat even on Mondays and fast on other days as well, like, for example, on the days of Saints Anastasie, Grigore, and Dumitru, some women even abstain from eating meat their whole lives, even though they don't wear monastic clothing.

Aside from this, the lower class in Moldavia, like in many other lands where select education did not yet enlighten, is inclined towards superstitions and did not get clean of the previous staining of mentioning unknown names from the Dacian cult during their songs, litanies, weddings, funerals, and other special occasions. Examples are Lado and Mano, Zîna, Drăgăica, Doina, Heoile, Stahia, Dracul în vale, Ursitele, Frumoasele, Sînzienele, Joimăriţile, Păpăluga, Chiraleisa, Colinda Turca, Zburătorul, Miază-Noapte, Striga, Tricolici, Legătura, Dezlegătura, Farmec, Disîntec, Vergelat, and others like these.[45]

---

[45] LADO and MANO, whose names are cited during weddings by women, bring a reasonable assumption that they refer to Venus and Cupido, the divinities of love and marriage.

ZÎNA (fairy), a word believed to come from the name Diana. However, they rarely use singular, mostly using the plural Zînele and say they're very beautiful girls who spill their charm on others.

DRĂGAICA seems to show the name of goddess Ceres. In truth, during the season when grains start to mature, all the girls in neighboring villages gather and choose the most beautiful one among them, naming her Drăgaică. They adorn her with a crown of wheat and multiple masterfully embroidered veils, hang the granary keys on her wrists and accompany her with a great retinue to the fields. Drăgaica thus adorned, reaches her arms up, holding the veils in the wind so that she seems to be flying and returns home from the field, going through every village singing and dancing, surrounded by all her sisters that often call her their sister and master in their songs. Moldavian peasant girls are very willing to accept this honor, even though an uninterrupted tradition says that the one playing the role of Drăgaica won't be married for the next three years.

DOINA seems to have been the Dacian name for Mars or Bellona because with it start all the songs recalling brave war deeds and all the introductions Moldavians use in songs.

HEOILE are found in wailing songs, not as an interjection, but as a certain person.

STAHIA they imagine as a woman with a giant body, who guards old abandoned houses, especially the underground ones, even treasures.

DRACUL ÎN VALE (Devil in the Valley): this is what they name the demons they think live in water.

URSITELE (the fates) they believe to be two girls who are present when a child is born, willingly gifting him with soul and body attributes, predestining everything good and bad that must happen during his life.

FRUMOASELE (the Beautiful) they believe to be nymphs of the sky, who are often in love with handsome young men. For this reason, if a young man suddenly becomes paralyzed, they believe this harm was done by them and it's the way they punish the men's disobedience, transforming love into hate and fury.

SÎNZIENELE is the name given to John the Baptist. They're convinced that in the day this saint is celebrated, the sun doesn't follow its path smoothly like usual, but trembles. That's why all the peasants in Moldavia wake up before the sun comes up and watch the sunrise closely; because the eye can't stand its light, it moves and trembles, movement that they believe in be the sun, and they return home happily.

JOIMĂRIȚELE: that's what they call the women believed to roam through houses with fires blazing in the fireplace during Maundy Thursday before Easter; it's believed that if they find a woman sleeping they punish her so that she won't be able to work anymore.

PĂPĂLUGA: during the summer when crops are threatened by drought, peasants in Moldavia dress up a girl under ten years old, in tree leaves and other weeds. Behind her come all the other children of the same age, singing and dancing in all the surrounding villages, and when they reach their destination, the custom asks for old women to pour cold water on their heads. Their song sounds like this: "Păpălugă, fly in the sky, open their gates and let the rain free, so the wheat and millet may grow" etc.

CHIRALEISA originates in the conjuration of Κύριε ἐλησον, used in Christian prayers. In truth, on February fifth when lights are turned on, all households make a wooden cross that they dress nicely in white fabric, silk and a long dress, depending on everyone's possibilities, and after vespers, they carry it in a procession at every house, surrounded by a big group of children shouting as often as they can *Chiraleisa*.

COLINDA corresponds to old Roman calendars and is celebrated through different traditions at the beginning of every year by all Moldavians, both boyars and peasants.

ȚURCA is a dance said to have been invented in the old times driven by hatred towards the Turks. During the holiday of Christ's birth, they take a stag head with big antlers, tie a mask to it and a striped cloth long enough to cover the feet of the one meant to wear it. On top of this made-up creature, climbs another person, wearing a mask that resembles a hunched old man, and in this manner, they roam the streets and houses, jumping and dancing.

ZBURĂTORUL (the flyer) is, they believe, a beautiful man that breaks into the girls' rooms, especially wives that recently got married, without being seen by others, even though they stay on the lookout for him, and taint their nights with forbidden love. But I heard that some married men, whom Prometheus made their innards from better clay, caught some of these flying Gods, and after realizing they are beings with human body, they gave them the deserved punishment.

MIAZĂ-NOAPTE (midnight) is said to be a ghost that wanders the crossroads from sunset to midnight, taking the face of different beings and disappearing after that.

STRIGA, from the Greek word στρίγλη. In Moldavia it means the same thing as it meant to Romans, an old witch that kills newborns through devilish powers, but it's unknown how she does it. This superstition is spread among Transylvanians, because they say that healthy children are found lifeless in their cribs while the striga wanders about.

If they suspect any hag of this doing, they bind her hands and legs and throw her into a river, and if she sinks, they declare her innocent, but if she floats, they consider this is the only proof they need, and burn her alive without trial, no matter how much she shouts her innocence until she gives her last breath.

TRICOLICI is the same thing as the French Loup garou; they believe some people can turn into wolves or other predators and that they adopt their natures, so that they end up ripping apart people and animals.

LEGĂTURA (tie) is a kind of spell through which they say the groom is prevented from getting near his bride. The same way they believe wolves and other wild animals can be prevented from causing damage to herds of sheep and cattle.

DEZLEGĂTURA (untie) is the untying of the charm above through other magic, which they think can be acquired through strong witchcraft.

FARMECUL (charm) is a kind of spell that peasants usually do, through which women think they are able to keep their lovers close or madden the ones they hate.

DESCÎNTECUL is another type of charm they say cures any illness that's not fatal. I won't hesitate to tell you what I've seen myself regarding this, at our own home.

The head of the *cămărași* at my father's home had a beautiful horse that got bitten by a field snake, and its body swelled up so badly nobody believed it would make it. An old witch that got summoned commanded the owner of the horse to find a spring, and bring a cup of water from it, a cup that nobody drank from. When he wanted to send a servant to bring the water, the old woman stopped him and told him the water must be brought by the owner himself, if he wants his horse to live. Finally, the young man listened and brought her a big jug of water. The old woman charmed the water in I don't know what manner, and then gave it to the young man to drink all of it. He obeyed, but not easily, because he had brought too much water. After he finished drinking, he saw his horse that was laying half dead on the ground starting to breathe, and he felt his own body swelling up and was tormented by pains he could barely endure. As soon as the old woman repeated the incantations, the horse recovered in less than fifteen minutes, and the young man threw the water back out and stopped feeling any type of pain.

I know that another old woman once cured all the horses in the stables that had mange, even though she lived three days away and did her witchcraft using a few horse hairs.

VERGELAT is a type of riddle played during the night before New Year's Day, through which Moldavians try to guess the lucks or troubles they would face during the year, by using a certain setting of sticks. For this purpose, they use fibers of bark from linden trees (tiliae), seeds (fabae) and pots (ollae) set in a certain order.

Chapter II
About the Church Hierarchy

Things outside of Moldavia's Church are in the ruler's charge; he eagerly watches over everyone so that the doings and teachings of the clerics correspond to the precepts of the Orthodox Church, and so none of them stray from the truth or, dressed in sheep's skin to hide a wolf's heart; he also watches for the shepherds not to abandon their flock or to cause scandals through their bad example. The spiritual path through which they lead souls to heaven was put in the Metropolitan's charge who, as a loyal shepherd and a restless subject of God, searches the churches in his submission, gives them bishops without much learning but full of the Holy Spirit, and doesn't reject anything he seems might be food and salvation for his sheep.

For this, however, because the population of Moldavia was increasing, considered this burden was too heavy for just one person to carry and to help him, they established three bishop seats: in Roman, Rădăuți, and Huși; from these, only the ones from Rădăuți and from Huși were given the titles of bishops, the one from Roman was given the title of "archbishop," and he was allowed to wear a miter during the liturgy; however, he has no jurisdiction over his other colleagues, and he's not superior to them in any way but his priority.

From the founding of the seat until the time of the Council of Florence, the Metropolitan of Moldavia received his ordination from the Patriarch of Constantinople. But because at that council, the Metropolitan, as a simple man without much knowledge of the holy scriptures, signed the deceiving orders of that synod, disregarding the opposition of Alexander the Good's envoys that were accompanying him to help him obtain the honor of the seventh throne promised to him by the Pope, and because after the priest assembly scattered, he didn't dare to return to Moldavia. Therefore, Marcu, the archbishop of Efes, named his archdeacon as Moldavia's Metropolitan, who was a Bulgarian, but well known for his godliness and faith, and because even the Patriarch of Constantinople was considered an enemy, he was ordered to request his confirmation from the Patriarch of Ohrid. From then until the end of the last century, Moldavia's metropolitans usually requested their blessings from the Patriarch in Ohrid.

But after Vasile Lupu took control of the country and started to straighten Moldavia's state of decay caused by his predecessors' indifference or the discords among them, Partenie, who was at the time the Patriarch of Constantinople, sent him a letter saying: "Your Highness knows that the Church of Moldavia obeyed the Eastern Church in the past like it was a good and true mother of all Christians and that its Metropolitan, like all the others, received his blessing from the ecumenical seat of Constantinople. It remained under this obedience for a few centuries, until during John Palaiologos's rule, the false Patriarch Mitrofan signed the ordinances of the Council of Florence, and through this, he obviously shook the trust of everyone who loved the true faith, even the first ecumenical seat of Constantinople. But after these troubles, because the ones who started this plague soon perished, the Holy Church, the righteous bride of God's groom, recovered its peace and brilliance from before, and any cause of suspicion towards it was removed, we consider it a serious and inappropriate thing for the Moldavian Church, that was always considered one of the select and notable parts of the Catholic Church, to not receive the blessing of ordination from the supreme seat, but from a lower one.

For that, our holy and humble synod, asks Your Highness, with reverence, to bring an honorable seat again to this honest part of the Church, and order the Metropolitan of Moldo-Wallachia (because that's how Greeks call Moldavia) to request again, as it was done in olden times, the blessing of our ecumenical seat and the Patriarchal one; this will be fully for God's glory and the honor of our mother, the Catholic Church." Urged by the Patriarch's letter and the synod, Vasile decided that from then forward the Metropolitan of Moldavia must only receive his blessing from the seat of Constantinople; this thing was strengthened by an ordinance of all patriarchs, accepted and signed even by the Patriarch of Ohrid, by the provincial synod that was held in Iași during the time of the same ruler against the iconoclasts and other heretics of that time.

As a matter of fact, the Metropolitan of Moldavia has a rank in the Eastern Church that others don't have. If he doesn't enjoy the title of Patriarch, he's neither a subject of any Patriarch. Even though he receives his blessing from the Patriarch of Constantinople, he can't be chosen by him, neither removed from his position nor forced like all the other metropolitans to wait for the ψήφος (approval) of the great Constantinople Church. Above the one who was chosen, after receiving the ruler's approval, three bishops of Moldavia set their hands, and after sending a letter to the Patriarch, they inform him that such and such named, a devout man, honest and learned, was chosen with the will of the Holy Spirit and not in any other way that depended on the will of any man. The ruler does the same through a letter to the Patriarch, asking him to strengthen the newly chosen one with his blessing, a thing the Patriarch cannot refuse in any way, but must fully obey the ruler's wish. He is also exempted from paying the tax called a contribution κοινότητος καί βοηθείας [for community and help] by all metropolitans, and he's not forced by any law to ask the Patriarch about what his duties are or what was done so far in Moldavia's Church but has the same freedom in Moldavia as the Patriarch has in Ohrid in his diocese; even if the Metropolitan enjoys so much respect, he cannot appoint or remove any of his bishops. Only the ruler has the right to inquire about the behavior and knowledge of the candidates for the bishop seats, to judge the guilt of those who must be removed from their positions, and pass the sentence for it. The rulers retained on their behalf all these rights and left only the ordination for the Metropolitan, according to the apostles' canons.

In turn, the ruler, even if he has absolute power over all his subjects, can't however change anything about how the Church is run, add or remove anything without the Metropolitan's consent. But this rule is only acknowledged by pious rulers; if any of them disregards the holy order, the Metropolitan's duty is to strengthen the ruler's decisions in the judgment seat according to the law; the ruler, as a good Christian and a lover of justice, submits to that.

The bishops have free will in their duties in their dioceses, appoint priests who submit to them, and if any is found to be at fault for something, they take his gift without anyone being able to oppose it;

but they have no right to name or dispose of abbots and archimandrites because they only obey the ruler. For lesser offenses, everyone gets punished by their superior: the deacon by the priest, the priest by the dean, the hieromonk and the monk by his abbot or by the archimandrite, the dean, abbot, and archimandrite by his bishop, the bishop by the Metropolitan, the Metropolitan by the ruler, and the ruler by his conscience and by God, who sometimes uses the Sultan as a mean to punish him. When it comes to more serious offenses that have to be punished by death or by dismissal, only simple priests, hieromonks, and monks are judged by their bishops, while abbots, archimandrites, and bishops can only be punished by the ruler. However, it is the bishops' duty that if any of those removed from the ruler's judgment commit something against the canons or cause unrest to bring it to the Metropolitan's attention through a letter, who then brings it to the ruler as it was presented by the bishop.

Year after year, the Metropolitan receives a tax of two hundred *aspri* from every priest in his diocese and a fox or ferret fur, and aside from these, he can't ask for anything else, the same way he gets no income from the bishops unless they willingly gift him with something. The bishops collect the same taxes from their diocese.

Chapter III
About the Monasteries of Moldavia

All the monasteries in Moldavia have the same structure and follow the laws written for monks by Saint Basil. There are only four big monasteries led by an archimandrite, but there are over two hundred smaller monasteries that obey abbots, and almost as many settlements subordinated to other monasteries that exist all over the place. They are divided into ἀφιερόμενα, subdued monasteries, and ἐλεύθερα, which are the free monasteries; the subdued monasteries are dedicated to Jerusalem, or to the Sinai Mount, or to Mount Athos. Because in Moldavia it is customary that if the ruler or a boyar wants to establish a monastery, he must share his fortune equally between the monastery and his children, and give the monastery as much as he gives to each of his children.

If he fears the monastery might collapse or be ruined after his death, he puts it under the authority of other greater monasteries that are found in the places I mentioned above. After this, the archimandrites of these lavras must preside over the monastery and make sure that the monks there live an immaculate life and have good habits. In return, from the monastery's incomes, they only leave enough for the monks' food, the rest they collect for the needs of the bigger lavras, money they send there each year; in a free monastery, however, the monks plow, sow, and harvest for their own needs, and during the hours they're not busy with religious services, they deal with various manual labors decided by the abbot, work in the vineyard, the fields, or the gardens, and the crops harvested by them are used for the monastery.

All monasteries pay a yearly tax to the ruler depending on how rich they are, but the Metropolitan and the bishop are exempted from taxes. It's known that all monks follow the rules of Saint Basil so tightly that they'd rather die than put any small piece of meat in their mouths, even if the doctor ordered them to do so. They never leave the monastery unless they're sent by the abbot or when they're allowed to leave for certain days or hours.

The management of the monastery is given to the older monks that earned the abbot's trust through their honesty and good habits, proven for many years. Besides this, we can't omit to praise the hospitality given by all the monasteries of Moldavia. Any person that came there as a guest, no matter if they're Orthodox, Jewish, Turkish, or Armenian, not only that they're received with kindness, but if they wanted to remain there for a whole year, they must be fed and taken care of together with their companions and their animals, without any complaint.

Chapter IV
About the Language of Moldavia

Writers have different opinions about the origins of the Moldavian language: many believe that it is an altered language that originated from Latin, without having had anything to do with another idiom; others believe that it is derived from the Italian dialect. I will be unbiased when exposing the arguments of some and others so that the truth would be better represented to the reader. The ones that claim that Latin was the true mother of the Moldavian language, base their assumptions on the following grounds: first, they say that the Roman colonies were brought to Dacia long before the Roman language was changed in Italy as a result of the Vandal invasions; no historian mentions anywhere that they returned to Latin during barbarian rule, meaning the people of Dacia couldn't alter their language with one that didn't yet exist.

Second, Moldavians were never called Italians, a name which started being used by other Romans in further lands in the times that followed, but they always kept their name of Romans during a time when Rome was the capital of the whole world. The fact that their Polish and Hungarian neighbors call them *vlah* doesn't mean anything, because that's how they commonly name Italians also. Actually, I prefer to believe that these neighboring nations took this name from Moldavians, because they were better known to them, and gave it to the Italians as well, not the other way around.

The third and strongest argument in favor of this opinion is that in the Moldavian language many Latin words are commonly found today, words that Italian doesn't know at all and, on the other side, Moldavian doesn't know any verbs and nouns that entered the Italian language through the Goths, Vandals, and Lombards. To make this clearer, the Italian shows *incipio* (to begin) through the barbaric *commincio*, while the Moldavian through the word *încep*, originated from altered Latin; *albus* (white) in Italian is *bianco*, while in Moldavian is *alb*; *civitas* (city) in Italian is *città*, and in Moldavian is *cetate*; *dominus* (ruler) in Italian is *signore*, while in Moldavian is *domn*; *mensa* (table) in Italian is *tavola*, Mold. *masă*; *verbum* (word), Ital. *parola*, Mold. *vorbă*; *caput* (head) Ital. *testa*, Mold. *cap*; *venatio* (hunt) Ital. *caccia*, Mold. *vânat*.

In turn, the ones that say Moldavian language derived from Italian point to the following ideas: 1. That in Moldavian are found the auxiliary verbs *am, ai, are*; 2. Numerical articles; 3. Even a few pure Italian words, for example, *șchiop* (lame), Ital. *sciopo* and *cerc* (circle) Ital. *cerco*, are words completely unknown to the Latin language, which couldn't have been taken from anywhere else other than from Italian.

To these, the supporters of the first opinion respond: Moldavians indeed use auxiliary verbs, however, they are not Italian, but words of their own. The same idea applies to articles because no other part of speech from Moldavian differs more from Italian than these. The Italian sets the article in front of the name, the Moldavian after it, for example, Ital. *l'huomo, la moglie*, Mold. *omul* (the man), *muierea* (the woman). Italian only uses a masculine article for singular which is *il*, and *gli* or *i* for plural, and feminine article *la* for singular and *le* for plural. Moldavians, however, have two articles for masculine singular, *ul* and *le*, one which they add to names ending in a consonant and the other to the names ending in vowels, for example, *omul* (the man), *calul* (the horse), *scaunul* (the chair), *vasul* (the bowl), *șarpele* (the snake), *cînele* (the dog), etc. For the plural of words representing beings, they add the article *i*, for example, *caii*, *oamenii*, and names of inanimate objects end with the feminine article *ele*, like *scaunele*, *vasele*, etc. For feminine words, Moldavians also use two articles, *e* and *a*, for example, *muiere* (woman), *găina* (hen). The ones ending in *e* change their plural to *ile*, like *muiere- muierile*, and the ones ending in *a* change their plural to *ele*, like *găina- găinele*.

Finally, those words that resemble Italian more than they resemble the old Roman language, can be believed, through a supposition that isn't a bit absurd, to have infiltrated our language through a long trade with the Genovese, during the times when they ruled the shores of the Black Sea. In the same way, after Moldavians started to do business with the Greeks, Turks, and Poles, in their language started to be heard more words from the languages of these nations, as the following Greek examples show:

Pedeapsă (punishment)	παίδευσις
Chivernisire (administration)	κυβέρνησις
Procopie (feat)	προκοπή
Blestem (curse)	βλασφημώ
Azimă (unleavened bread)	άξυμον
Drum (journey)	δρόμος
Pizmă (envy)	πεῖσμα

About the Language of Moldavia

Now, after I showed you the arguments of both sides, I don't dare to tell you which one of them gets closer to the truth, for fear that the love of my country might cloud my sight and hide things that other eyes could uncover easier. We leave this judgment for the reader and refer only to what Covantius said. It's curious, he says, that the language of Moldavians and Wallachians contains more Latin words than Italian, even though the Italians live on the same lands where the Romans used to live. But this is not such a wonder. Italians formed their language much later. As a matter of fact, it can be observed that the Moldavian language contains a few words that, being unknown to the Latin language or to the languages of their neighbors, I believe, maybe not without reason, that they have remained from the language of old Dacia. In truth, nothing prevents us from believing the Roman colonies used Dacian slaves, or even if someone lost their wife, or took a wife of that nation, from where native words could have slipped into their language easily. Some of these words are *stejar* (oak tree), *pădure* (forest), *heleșteu* (pond), *cărare* (path), *grăiesc* (speak), *privesc* (watch), *nemeresc* (hit).

Aside from these, like in almost all other languages, the Moldavian language has various dialects. The purest language is used in the middle of Moldavia, in the lands of Iași, because the residents of this area, being in the constant presence of the royal court, are more polished than the others. The ones living along the river Dniester mix in their speech many Polish words and call different dishes used in households using Polish names, so they're hard to understand by other Moldavians. The ones living in the mountains towards Transylvania use Hungarian words often, the ones from Fălciu alternate

Moldavian language with the Tartar one, and the ones from Galați mix it with Greek and Turkish.

Even Moldavian women have a different pronunciation that differs from the one men use. They change the syllabus *bi* and *vi* to *ghi*, for example, *bine- ghine* (good), *vie- ghie* (vineyard); they change *pi* to *chi*, for example, *pizmă- chizmă* (envy), *piatra- chiatra* (rock); *m* initially changes to *ng*, hard to pronounce by others, for example, *mie- ngie* (mine). Whoever got used to this pronunciation, even the men, can't wean themselves off of using it, and give themselves away like mice for spending too much time at their mother's breast, which is why they're normally mocked and called "sons of hags" (*feciori de babă*)

The inhabitants of Wallachia and Transylvania have the same language as Moldavians, but their pronunciation is harsher so that *giur* the Wallachian will pronounce *jur*, through a Polish *z* or a French *j*; *Dumnedzău* (God), Val. *Dumnezeu*; *acum* (now), Val. *acuma*; *acela* (that), Val. *ahăla*. They even introduced a few words unknown to Moldavians that they avoid using in writing. They follow the Moldavian language and spelling, admitting through this that the Moldavian language is cleaner than their own, even if the enmity between Wallachians and Moldavians prevents them from admitting it openly.

The language that the Cuțovlahi use, the ones living in Rumelia on the border with Macedonia, is way more deformed. They mix strangely their native tongue with Greek and Albanian, so that they sometimes introduce in the Wallachian language pure Greek words, sometimes Albanian ones, but always keep the Moldavian inflections for nouns and verbs. Among themselves, they understand their mash, but neither the Greek, the Albanian, nor the Moldavian can fully understand their speech. If all three were gathered together however and heard the Cuțovlah speaking, and each translated a phrase for the others, they could understand what he wanted to say by putting them all together.

Chapter V

About Moldavian Letters

Before the Council of Florence, following the example of the other nations whose languages originate from the Roman language, Moldavians used Latin characters. But after that synod, the Metropolitan of Moldavia switched to the papist side and, as I said above, his successor, the deacon of Marcu of Efes, who was a Bulgarian named Teoctist, in order to eliminate every papist seed from the Moldavian Church and to take away the chance for Moldavian youth to read papist sophistry, he advised Alexander the Good to banish everyone who had another point of view when it came to the Church, also to get rid of Latin letters and replace them with Slavic ones; through this exaggerated and improper zeal, he was the initiator of this cruelty that now rules Moldavia. But because Slavic letters weren't enough to express the pronunciation of all words that Moldavian borrowed from Latin and the other neighboring nations, they had to make up a few new letters, so Moldavian ended up having a higher number of letters than any other European language. Today the number of letters together with a few other prosodic and orthographic symbols is forty-seven:

| *Az* | *Ije* | *Tferd* |
| *BukI* | *I* | *Uc* |

About Moldavian Letters

Vede	*Kako*	*U*
Glagol	*Liude*	*Ferta*
Dobro	*Mislete*	*Fita*
Iest	*Naş*	*Hier*
E	*On*	*Hier*
Jivete	*Pocoi*	*Ier [mic]*
Dzealo	*Rîţi*	*Ieri*
Zemle	*Slovo*	*Ier*

This *ier* always concluded a word ending in a consonant, today however Moldavians use a sign in its place, put above as in the word *iert*.

Ot	*Ştea*	*Iu*
O	*Iat*	*Xi*
Ţi	*Ie*	*Psi*
Cerv	*Înea*	*Titla*
Şa	*Iako*	*Ge*

Capital letters in Moldavian are the same used by Greeks and Slavs in their alphabets; in truth, both types of letters are used the same way.

The letters I showed you, Moldavians started using in family letters and personal signatures after the Latin letters were removed, but in holy books, rulers' letters, treasury registers, and other court records, no other language was used for two centuries except Slavic. That's why the sons of boyars only learned Slavic, and because other sciences can't be taught in it after they learned how to read, they had to memorize the Oriental Church breviary, the Octoechos, and the Psalter. After finishing these lessons, they were taught the Gospel, the apostles' writings, and Pentateuch, rarely the other books of the Old Testament, and only as much as to understand what the Holy Bible consists of. All the boyars' daughters learned the same things, to to read and write the country's language. It was rare to find someone that strived to learn Slavic, especially Slavic grammar, collected by Maxim Cretanul, who Moldavians set among the saints, which was edited only once in Moscow and is very hard to find.

But in the last century, during the reign of Vasile Lupu, when the ecumenical seat was restored, Moldavia started to wake up and get out of the deep darkness the barbarians covered it with. Through the care of this ruler, a Greek school was founded in Iași, and he ordered all the monasteries to take in Greek monks in order to teach boyars' sons their writings and teachings. He was also the one who ordered a second choir for the Metropolitan church, one formed of Greek cantors, in honor of the Patriarchal church, and for the whole liturgy to be served half in Greek and half in Slavic as it is done today.

The same ruler brought Greek and Moldavian typography, ordering church books and codices to be printed, which was followed by the Bible to be read in the country's language, then the apostle, and finally the whole liturgy.

A few decades later, the ruler of Wallachia, Șerban Cantacuzino, followed the pious deeds of Vasile and founded schools, and Greek, and Romanian typography in his country. Finally, towards the end of the last century, some Moldavians started to learn Latin and sciences. Giving a good example to the others, the path was opened by Miron, a logofăt, the most conscientious historian of Moldavia, who sent his sons to Poland to get schooled in Latin and the liberal arts. After him, Duca, the ruler of Moldavia, summoned a young scholar to teach his sons, named John Papas (who later took the name of Comnenus in Moscow and finally was appointed to the Metropolitan seat of Drista). He also summoned the hieromonk Cigala. Our father, Constantine Cantemir, called on the great hieromonk scholar named Ieremia Cacavela Cretanul and charged him with teaching his sons and the sons of other boyars; since then more and more Moldavians started to learn Greek, Italian, and Latin words.

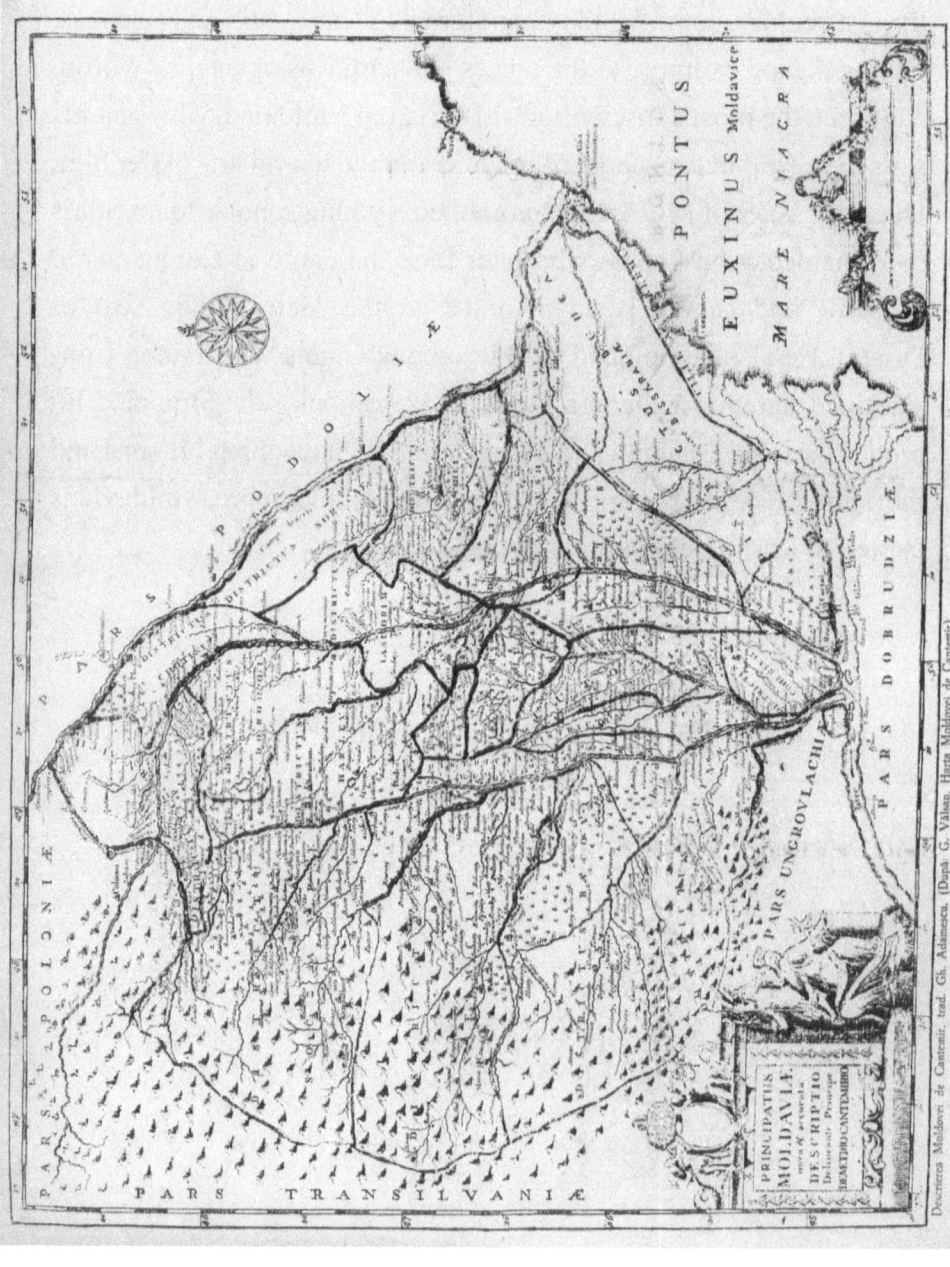

Descrierea Moldovei de Cantemir, trad. Gh. Adamescu. (După G. Vâlsan, Harta Moldovei de Cantemir).

Index

A

Abazeștii, 178
Abkhazians, 177
acchiulahlîi, 101
Achileea. See Chilia
Adjud, 34
Aeneas Sylvius, 175
Aga, 129
agalari, 93, 97
Akkerman, 29, 42, 44, 51, 125
alagari, 101
Alba Iulia. See Cetatea Albă
Albanians, 140, 168, 185
alem, 103, 145
Alexander the Good, 68, 74, 85, 222, 234
Alexander I, 74, 75, 115, 123, 157
Alexander IV, 115
Alexander, son of Roman I, 74
Anastasie, 216
Antonie Roset, 82
Arăpeștii, 178
Arbureștii, 178
archimandrite, 225, 226
armaș, 129, 132, 161
armășei, 138
Armenians, 46, 78, 109, 185, 187, 227
Aron, 79
arzodasî, 91
Asan, 178
Ascension, 199
aspri, 133, 153, 167, 225
Athos Mountain, 226
auroch, 18, 47, 61

B

Babadag, 118
Bacău, 42, 53, 54, 132, 165, 215
bacșiș, 153
Bahce-Kapu, 94
Bahlui River, 28, 31, 32
Bahluieț, 28
Bai-i-humaiun, 97
Bănilă River, 27
Bârlad, 26, 27, 33, 34, 125
Bârlad River, 26, 27, 34
barley, 55
Barnovski, Miron, 80, 84, 109, 115
baș-bakyculi, 121
Bașbuluc-bașa, 140
Bașeu, 28, 60
Basil the Great, 149, 216
Basilicale, 158
Bașoteștii, 178
Bathie, 32
Bayezid II, Sultan, 24, 69
bees, 62
Bellona, 217
Bender, 22, 26, 37, 79, 118
Berheci, 27
Berheci River, 57
beșli, 141
beșli-agasî, 104
Bessarabia, 20, 22, 23, 28, 29, 31, 35, 42, 57, 58, 62, 125, 128, 191, 194
bezmăn, 136
Bîcovăț, 28
Bîcu, 28
Bicu River, 22
big mucarer, 113
Bîrlad, 165

Bîrlădeț, 27
Bistrița River, 27, 42
bitumen, 54
Black Sea, 22, 25, 26, 35, 44, 49, 230
Bogdan, 18, 61, 67, 74, 76, 78, 108, 109, 139, 170
Bogdan cel Orb, 69
Bogdan II, 75
Bogdan III, 108, 139
Bogdan V, 79
Bogdăneștii, 178
Bogdanli, 19
boiarski, 177
boiernași, 134, 182
Boliare, 123
Bonfinius, 33
Bontășeștii, 178
Botna River, 22, 27
Botoșani, 40, 164
boyars, 42, 70, 77-82, 84-87, 89, 90, 94, 97, 98, 102, 104-107, 109, 111, 113, 115, 116, 118, 120, 123, 124, 126, 127, 129, 130, 132, 134, 135, 137-139, 145-150, 153-155, 159-169, 171, 176-178, 181-188, 190, 193, 197, 198, 201, 202, 205, 208, 219, 226, 236, 237
Brâncoveanu, Constantin, 82, 83
Braniște, 127
Brateș Lake, 28
Buceag, 42, 43, 53, 58, 62, 191
Bucovina, 58
Bugeac, 27, 28, 128, 191
Buhușeștii, 178
Bulgarians, 123, 140, 168, 176, 185

C

cadiascheri, 98
caftan, 89, 93, 99, 102, 106, 111, 112, 172, 183
Cahul, 28
caimacami, 104, 116-118, 120
Căldărușa, 28
cale premare, 205
Călmățui, 28
călușari, 198, 199
Calvin, 215
cămărași, 133-136, 182, 183
Camenița, 26, 39, 53
căminar, 130
Caminca, 28
Camnița, 81
Câmpulung, 22, 59, 168
Cantacuzino, Dumitrașcu, 82
Cantacuzino, Șerban, 237
Cantemir, 167, 179
Cantemir, Antioh, 82, 83
Cantemir, Constantin, 34, 82, 83, 116, 237
Cantemir, Dimitrie, 82, 83
Cantemir, Theodor, 166
capugi-bașa, 102, 112, 113, 116-118, 120, 121, 129, 174
capugilar-chehaiasî, 91, 111
Cărăbățeștii, 179
Cârligătura County, 32, 35
Carpeștii, 179
Cașin, 27
Catargieștii, 179
Ceahlău, 50, 52
Ceaureștii, 179
ceauși, 93, 97, 102-104, 106, 112, 137, 145, 146
ceaușlar-emini, 93
Cerchizeștii, 179
Ceremuș River, 22, 27, 51
Ceres, 217
Cernăuți, 40, 60, 125, 126, 164
Cetatea Albă, 20, 26, 29
chehaia, 91, 93, 97, 98, 102, 110, 116, 121, 174
Chilia, 22, 42, 45, 57, 77, 115, 125, 166
chiliarhi, 106
Chiraleisa, 218
Chiur, 28
Choniates, Nicetas, 67, 178
Chrysopyle, 94
Cigala, 237
Cîmpulung, 165, 190, 191
Ciobăneștii, 179
Ciogoleștii, 179
ciohodar, 102, 135
Ciorna, 28
Circassians, 177, 179
Ciuclucul Mijlociu, 28
Ciulucul-Mare, 28
Ciulucul-Mic, 28
cîzlar-agasî, 91, 173
clucer, 128, 131
Cogîlnic River, 28
colăcari, 202

Index   241

Colacin Lake, 29
Colacin River, 22, 28, 29
Colinda, 219
Comis, 127
comnis, 131, 133, 137
conac, 104
Constantine the Great, 214
Constantinople, 21, 25, 26, 35, 59, 68,
    82, 90, 94, 96, 101, 102, 104, 106,
    107, 112, 116, 118, 120, 126, 142,
    157, 171, 177, 179, 187, 189, 215,
    222, 223
Corod, 27
Corovia, 28
Costacheștii, 179
Costești, 57
Costineștii, 179
Coțman, 28
Cotnari, 56, 57, 126
Covantius, 231
Covurlui, 35, 165
Cracău River, 27
Crasna, 27
Crimea, 37, 43, 53, 75, 126, 128, 138,
    191
cubbe, 98
cuca, 99, 101, 103, 109
Cuciur, 28
Cula, 28, 29
cupar, 135, 136
Cupido, 217
Curopalates, 124
Cuțovlahi, 232, 233
Czechs, 57

D

Dacia, 18, 24, 41, 48, 50, 67, 69, 157,
    175, 176, 213, 214, 228, 231
Dacia Alpestris, 18
Dacia Mediterranea, 18
Dacia Ripensis, 18
Dacians, 17, 19, 49, 157, 213, 217, 231
Dajuba, 213
danț, 197
Danube River, 18, 20, 22, 23, 25, 26,
    28, 29, 35, 46, 47, 56, 120, 170, 173,
    187
Danzig, 60
darabani, 130, 145
Darieștii, 179

David, 148
Decebal, 17, 49, 157, 175
Delia, 28
Descîntecul, 220
Dezlegătura, 220
Diana, 217
dieci, 127
Dinastris. See Dniester River
divan, 86, 87, 97, 98, 105-107, 113,
    118, 124, 127, 131-135, 137, 149,
    150, 159-164, 182, 183, 208
divan-effendisi, 119
Długosz, 190
Dniester River, 22, 25-29, 37-39, 44,
    52, 61, 128, 231
Dobrușa, 28
Docolina, 27
Doina, 217
Doneștii, 179
Doniceștii, 179
Dorohoi, 29, 39, 125, 165
Dorohoi Lake, 29
Dracul în vale, 218
Drăgaică, 217
Dragoș, 18, 61, 67, 73, 83, 157, 166,
    176, 187, 215
Drăgoșești, 69, 74, 76, 77, 79, 84, 187
Dragutețtii, 179
Drista, 237
Duca, 81, 82, 237
Dumbrăvile Roșii, 58
Dumitru, 216
Duraceștii, 179
dvoriane, 177

E

earthquakes, 21
Efes, 222, 234
Egypt, 21, 35, 214
Elan, 28
Europe, 21, 171
Eustratie Dabija, 116

F

Făclii, 167
Falcău, 56
Fălciu, 60, 232
Fanar, 94

Faraon River, 27
Farmecul, 220
ferîia, 165
Florence, 222, 234
Florence, Council of, 68, 74
Focșani, 34, 193
forests, 26, 42, 55, 57, 58, 62, 152, 153, 167, 200
Forum Romanorum. See Roman, town
Frățițeștii, 179
French, 121, 197, 219, 232
frumoasele, 199, 218
fustași, 142

G

Galați, 21, 25, 28, 34, 35, 104, 107, 112, 118, 142, 164, 232
Găneștii, 179
Gârla Mare, 28
Gașpar, 80
Gavrilițeștii, 179
Gedanum. See Danzig
gelepi, 187
Genovese, 230
Georgius Codinus, 124
Germans, 140, 168, 185
Germany, 25
Gerul Sohului River, 27
Ghica, Gheorghe, 81
gineceu, 134
glușca, 63
Goianeștii, 179
göller, 62
Goths, 229
Greci, 57
Greece, 96, 124, 176
Greeks, 44, 140, 168, 179, 185, 187, 223, 230, 235
Grigore, 216

H

Hăbășeștii, 179
Hadrian, 175
hasne-agasî, 171
hatman, 86, 89, 125, 140, 141
Heoile, 217
hieromonk, 225, 237
Hînceștii, 180

hînsari, 141
Hîrlău, 40, 56, 165
Hisăreștii, 180
hiucm ferman, 105
Hobîlna, 27
Horiata, 27
Horsa, 213
horses, 51, 55, 61, 97, 103, 112, 118, 120, 127, 137, 144, 148, 155, 170, 173, 189, 195, 196, 202, 203, 207, 220
Hotin, 22, 26, 39, 81, 142, 164
Hotin County, 52
Humor, 27
Hungarians, 22, 57, 61, 69, 139, 185, 186, 188, 215, 229, 232
Hungary, 18, 25, 48, 115, 215
husari, 141
Huși, 36, 56, 131, 221

I

Iachel, 28
Ialpug, 28, 42, 44, 47
Iancu Sasul, 171
Iași, 31, 32, 82, 101, 104, 106, 107, 112, 118, 120, 126, 129, 135, 141, 154, 163, 164, 186, 223, 231, 236
Iași County, 31, 33
Ichel River, 61
ici-agalarî, 93
iedeccii, 101
ieniceri-agasî, 98
Ieremia Cacavela Cretanul, 237
ieruncă, 63
ikindi, 98
Iliaș. See Ilie III
Ilie I, 75
Ilie III, 81
imbrohor, 93, 101
Ioan, miller, 31
Isăceștii, 180
ischiemne-agasî, 174
iskemne-agasî, 101
Ismail, 47, 57, 166
Italian, 23, 28, 30, 34, 58, 67, 69, 80, 228-231, 237
Italians, 19, 228, 231
Italy, 228
Iuga, 74
Iznovăț, 28

J

Jerusalem, 226
Jesus Christ, 105, 159
Jews, 46, 185-187, 196, 227
jidnicer, 131
Jijia, 28
Jijia River, 27-29
Jitnicier, 128, 133
John Albert, King of Poland, 24, 69
John the Evangelist, 216
John the Armenian, 115, 171
John Chrysostom, 216
John Paleologus, 74, 124, 222
John Papas, 237
John, Wallachian leader, 67
Joimăriţele, 218
Joreştii, 181

K

kapugilar-chehaiasî, 102
Kazakhs, 139, 140, 168, 185
Kazakhstan, 134
Kiriaceştii, 180
Kupalo, 213
Kyvirgic, 59

L

Lado, 213, 217
Lake Ovidius, 29
Lăpuşna, 28
Larga, 28
Laţco, 74
Latin, 78, 123, 175, 200, 228, 229, 231, 234, 236, 237
Laţiu, 228
Legătura, 220
leonines, 173, 174, 203
Leunclavius, 68
Lipcan Tartars, 140
Lithuania, 140
logofăt, 86, 87, 89, 124, 125, 129, 130, 136, 147, 148, 160, 162, 164, 183, 237
Lohan, 27
Lombards, 229
Lower Country, 125
Luther, 215

Lycostomon. See Chilia

M

maden-halfasi, 172
malaria, 21
Mano, 217
Maramureş, 48, 185
Marcu, 222, 234
Mars, 217
Matthias Corvinus, 23, 24, 69
Mavrocordat, Nicolae, 83
Maxim Cretanul, 236
mectupci-effendi, 172
medelnicer, 128, 131, 149, 151
Mereştii, 180
Messiah, 116, 117
Metropolitan, 32, 74, 87-89
Miază-Noapte, 219
Micleştii, 180
Mihuleştii, 180
Milcov River, 23, 27, 34, 57
Mileştii, 180
Milet, 28
millet, 55, 218
Mira Monastery, 34
miralem-aga, 97
miriahor, 102
Miron, 80, 84, 109, 115, 237
Mitrofan, 222
Mocosa, 213
Moineşti, 54
Molda, 18
Moldavia River, 27, 59
Moldo-Wallachia, 95
Molniţa River, 27
Moncastru, 125
Moscow, 236, 237
Moşna, 28
Moţoceştii, 180
Movilă, Ieremia, 79
Movilă, Simion, 79, 80
Movileşti family, 84, 140, 180
muftiu, 98
muhzur-agasî, 99
Munteni, 19
Murguleştii, 180

N

Năculeștii, 180
Nazarenes, 111
Nazars, 105
Neamț, 27
Neamț County, 50
Neculeștii, 180
Niceea, 148, 215
Nicorești, 57
Nirnova, 28

O

oats, 35, 55
Occident, 215
Oceakov, 22
Ocna, 42, 165
ocne, 53
Octoechos, 236
Odobești, 56
Ohrida, 223, 224
Oituz, 27
Olympus, 50
Orhei, 27, 29, 38, 61, 128, 164
Orichovius, Stanislas, 69
Orient, 215
Osliado, 213
Ottomans, 70-72, 80-84, 108, 109, 170
Ovid, 29, 45

P

paharnic, 86, 131, 132, 136, 149
păhărnicei, 135, 137, 145, 150
paici, 101, 103, 137
Paladieștii, 180
Palamas, 216
Paleologus, John, 68
Păpălugă, 218
pârcălab, 32, 40, 164-168, 179
Patriarch of Constantinople, 94, 96
Pelias, 50
Pentateuch, 236
Persians, 62, 186
Peruna, 213
peșcheș, 92, 96, 173, 174
pețitori, 200
Petralifii, 180
Peter, 171
Peter I Mușat, 74
Peter II, 74
Peter Rareș, 33, 69, 76, 77, 115
Peter V, 115
Peter VI, 115
Phrygian, 101, 103
Piasecius, 190
Piatra, 42, 142
pigs, 61, 167, 168
Pilateștii, 180
Pindus, 50
Pisoscheștii, 180
Pitar, 128, 131
pivnicer, 136
Pocuția, 63
Podolia, 61
Pohvist, 213
Poland, 21, 23, 26, 27, 29, 41, 44, 60, 78, 115, 142, 176, 188-190, 237
Poles, 19, 20, 22, 23, 32, 37, 39, 40, 44, 57, 58, 60, 61, 63, 68, 75, 79-81, 139, 142, 179, 180, 185, 188, 190, 197, 229-232
polihron, 96
Pope, 215, 222
postelnic, 86, 88, 89, 106, 107, 129, 130, 132, 145, 146, 150, 151, 159, 182-184
postelnicel, 182
Prajeștii, 180
Premisl, 190
primicer, 198
pristol, 88, 95
Prometheus, 219
Prut River, 18, 22, 25, 27-29, 31, 35, 40, 48, 58, 127, 128, 191
Psalter, 236
Putila, 27, 59
Putna, 23, 27, 34, 57, 59, 164, 190

R

Rabie, 36
Răcătău River, 27
Racova, 27, 167
Racoviță, 83, 167
Racoviță, Michael, 83
Racovițeștii, 180
Radu, Ruler of Moldavia, 32
Radul Lungul, 80
Rărăuți, 221

Răut River, 28, 29, 38, 61
Răutul River, 27
Razii, 180
Rebricea, 27
Rîşca, 27
Roman, 17, 29, 32, 42, 48, 67, 74, 75, 85, 133, 157, 158, 164, 175, 176, 187, 215, 219, 221, 228, 230, 231, 234
Roman County, 32
Roman Empire, 67
Roman I, 74, 85
Romans, 19, 44, 47, 50, 67, 176, 213, 219, 228, 231
Rome, 214, 228
Ropceneştii, 180
Rumelia, 232
Ruseteştii, 180
Russia, 134, 142, 187
Russians, 19, 39, 43, 47, 57, 59, 83, 142, 173, 177, 185, 186, 189, 213
Ruthenian, 188
rye, 55

S

Sacovăţ, 27
Saint Nicholas Church, 32
Saint Basil, 183, 226
Salcea, 28
salt, 35, 53, 128, 165, 167, 168
sangeac, 96, 145
sangiac, 109
sangiac-agasî, 103
sangiacdar, 98
Sărata, 28
Sărata River, 60
Sardanapal, 171
Sardica, 214
Sarnicius, 190
Sas, 74
său taht, 99
Serafineţ, 28
seraschier, 118
Serbians, 123, 140, 168, 176, 179, 185
serdar, 130, 131
Serdar, 128
Scythe, 196
Scythian, 36, 43, 213
Scythians, 17, 36, 58, 62, 67, 140, 177, 213

seimeni, 129, 140, 145
Semargle, 213
Sepoteneştii, 180
sheep, 51, 52, 59, 142, 167, 168, 187, 189, 190, 195, 215, 220, 221
silihtar, 98, 102
silihtar-agasî, 98
Silişteanul, 167
Sinai Mount, 226
Sînzienele, 218
Sîrca, 28
Siret River, 23, 25-28, 33-35, 40, 41, 57
Sireţel, 27
Sitna, 28
Slatina, 27
Slavic, 123
small mucarer, 113
Smedorova, 33
Smila, 27
Solca, 27
Soloneţ, 27, 28
Soroca, 38, 39, 59, 60, 128, 142, 164
spătar, 40, 86, 89, 131, 132, 145, 146, 149, 159, 162
spătărie, 107, 126, 135, 137
St. Nicholas, 104
Stahia, 217
stareţ, 198
staroste, 200
Stephen the Great, 21, 22, 24, 31, 33, 44, 57, 68, 69, 108, 115, 139, 166, 170
Stephen I, 74, 85
Stephen II, 74
Stephen III, 75
Stephen VII, 115
Stephen, son of Petru Rareş, 69
Stîrceştii, 180
stolnic, 131, 135, 149
Stolnic, 127
stolnicei, 138
Striba, 213
striga, 219
Strîmba, 28
Sturzeştii, 181
Suceava, 26, 31, 32, 40, 47, 125, 164, 190, 197
Suceviţa, 27
Suleiman, 41, 46, 76, 77, 98, 115
sulger, 131, 133
Sulger, 128

sutaşi, 106

Ş

şarhorodeni, 134
şatîri, 93, 102, 103
Şchiopul, 115, 171
Şeptiliceştii, 181
Şerbăneşti, 26
Şetrar, 128
Şoldaneştii, 181
Şomuzul River, 27
Ştefăneşti, 128
Şubana, 28
şugubinat, 196

T

tabulhanaua, 97
Taifs, 35
Tălăbeştii, 181
talhîş, 90, 110, 116
talhîşci, 110
Tălpeştii, 181
Tămăşeştii, 181
Tanschii, 181
tar, 54
Târgul Frumos, 32, 165
Tartar language, 19
Tartars, 22, 23, 27, 28, 34, 36, 37, 43, 48, 58, 61, 62, 80, 128, 140, 176-178, 189, 191, 194-196, 232
Tauric Chersonese, 179
Tăutuleştii, 181
Tazlău, 27, 50
Tazlău River, 51
Tazlău Sărat, 27, 54
Tecuci, 26, 34, 57, 164
tefterdar, 99, 172, 174
Teoctist, 234
Tigheci, 58, 167, 191
Tigheciu, 28, 57
Tighina, 37
Tohatin, 61
Tokai, 56
Topoliţa, 27
Totoeştii, 181
Traian, village, 22
Trajan, 17, 35, 48, 175

Transylvania, 18, 20, 22, 32, 42, 50, 79, 115, 171, 187, 215, 232
Tricolici, 219
Trotuş River, 23, 27, 42, 53, 132
Tudoreştii, 181
tui. See tuiuri
tuiuri, 96, 103
Turculeştii, 181
Turks, 19, 22, 23, 26, 37, 39, 41, 42, 44, 46, 47, 52, 57, 59, 61, 68, 75-84, 90, 92, 93, 96, 98, 100, 103, 104, 108-110, 112, 115, 118, 121, 122, 125, 129, 137-142, 145, 149, 150, 153, 159, 166, 168, 170, 171, 173, 176, 186, 187, 190, 195, 206, 219, 227, 230, 232
Turla. See Dniester River
Tutova, 27, 33, 57, 164
Tutova County, 33
Tutova River, 33
Tyras River. See Dniester River

Ţ

Ţarigrad, 142
Ţifeştii, 179
Ţurca, 219

U

Ukraine, 20
Ulpiu Trajan, 157
ungureni, 187
Upper Country, 39, 125
Ureche, 167
Urecheşti, 167
Urecheştii, 181
uricari, 129
Ursitele, 218
uşar, 129, 132
uşărei, 138

V

Valea Albă, 27
Valea Brătuleni, 28
Valea Mare, 28
Valea Neagră River, 27
Valea Rea, 27

vameş, 130
Vasile the Albanian, see Vasile Lupu
Vasile Lupu, 29, 81, 158, 178, 236
Vaslui, 27, 137, 165, 196
Vaslui County, 33
Vasluieţ, 27
vătaf, 134, 135, 137, 142, 143, 145, 149, 161
vecin, 187
Venetian, 46, 121, 170
Venus, 217
Vergelat, 220
Vespers, 203
Vilna, 27
Virgin Mary, 216
Vîrlăneştii, 181
vistier, 127, 131-133, 136, 137, 147, 169
vistiernic, 168, 169
vizier, 82, 90, 91, 93, 96-98, 102, 104, 109, 110, 112, 113, 116, 120, 122, 129, 172-174
vlah, 229

Volochs, 19
Volos, 213
vornic, 34, 125, 136, 141, 163, 165, 190
Vrancea, 34, 60, 190
Vrancea Mountains, 34, 60
Vulgata, 216

W

Wallachia, 18, 23, 34, 48, 50, 80-82, 97, 122, 139, 178, 190, 193
Wallachians, 19, 67, 170
Whitsuntide, 199

Z

Zaporozhian, 140
Zburătorul, 219
Zeletin, 27
Zînele, 217
Zorileştii, 181

CENTER FOR Romanian STUDIES

The mission of the Center for Romanian Studies is to promote knowledge of the history, literature, and culture of Romania to an international audience. For more information contact us at info@centerforromanianstudies.com

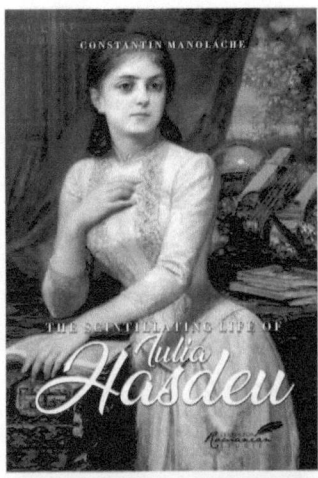
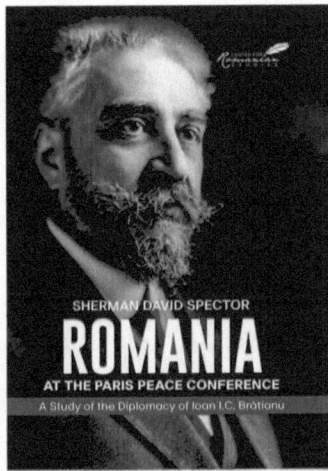

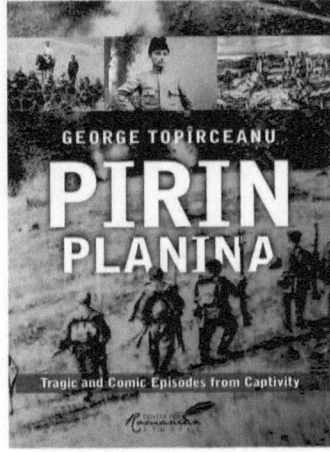

Check out these and other great titles at
CenterforRomanianStudies.com

www.ingramcontent.com/pod-product-compliance
Lightning Source LLC
Chambersburg PA
CBHW030442090526
44586CB00044B/537